CONCEPTS AND INQUIRY:
The Educational Research Council
Social Science Program

The Human Adventure

Medieval Civilization

Prepared by the Social Science Staff of the Educational
Research Council of America

ALLYN AND BACON, INC.

Boston   Rockleigh, N.J.   Atlanta   Dallas   Belmont, Calif.

THE *HUMAN ADVENTURE* SERIES WAS PREPARED BY THE
FOLLOWING MEMBERS OF THE SOCIAL SCIENCE STAFF OF
THE EDUCATIONAL RESEARCH COUNCIL OF AMERICA:

NANCY BOSTICK, CONSTANCE BURTON, NANCY HENDERSON,
MICHAEL JOYCE, MARILYN McLAUGHLIN, AGNES MICHNAY,
JAMES PACKARD, MARIE RICHARDS, MARY RITLEY, JUDITH WENTZ,
MARLENE ZWEIG.

MARY CATHERINE McCARTHY, EDITOR-IN-CHIEF

RAYMOND ENGLISH, DIRECTOR

The Educational Research Council of America acknowledges the contributions of the
Kettering Family Fund and the Martha Holden Jennings Foundation, which have made
possible the Social Science Program of the Educational Research Council of America.

Cover by Barry Zaid, Push Pin Studios, Inc.

Title page photograph by Giraudon.

CONTENTS

MAPS

ACKNOWLEDGMENTS

Preface — opposite p. 1, Scala (Biblioteca Laurenziana, Florence); p. 9, The City of Liverpool Museums; **Chapter 1** — p. 10, Editorial Photocolor Archives; p. 14 (top) Alan Band Associates, (bottom left) Magnum Photos, (bottom right) Arabian American Oil Company; p. 16, De Wys, Inc.; p. 20, Courtesy of the Museum of Fine Arts, Boston; p. 22 (left) Editorial Photocolor Archives, (right) Arabian American Oil Company; p. 25, Alan Band Associates; **Chapter 2** — p. 28, Editorial Photocolor Archives (Turkish-Islamic Museum); p. 41 (top left) The Toledo Museum of Art, (top right) The Smithsonian Institute, Freer Gallery of Art, Washington, D.C., (bottom) Carl E. Östman (Edith Henriksson); p. 42, Editorial Photocolor Archives; p. 43, Alan Band Associates; p. 45, De Wys, Inc.; p. 47, Alan Band Associates; **Chapter 3** — p. 48, R. B. Fleming; p. 52, De Wys, Inc.; p. 53, Alan Band Associates; p. 55, De Wys, Inc.; p. 58, Carl E. Östman; p. 63, R. B. Fleming; **Chapter 4** — p. 64, Editorial Photocolor Archives (Bargello Museum, Florence); p. 73, Alan Band Associates; p. 74 (left) The Metropolitan Museum of Art, Munsey Fund, 1932, (right) Giraudon (Reims Museum); p. 75 (left) The Metropolitan Museum of Art, Gift of Jean Jacques Reubell, 1926 in memory of his mother Julia C. Coster and of his wife, Adeline E. Post, both of New York City, (right) The Metropolitan Museum of Art, Gift of William H. Riggs, 1913; p. 78, Giraudon; p. 79, Editorial Photocolor Archives; p. 81, Giraudon; **Chapter 5** — p. 84, Lauros-Giraudon, p. 87, Courtesy of the Trustees of the British Museum, from the Luttrell Psalter; p. 91, Giraudon; p. 93, Weston Kemp/Perceval; p. 94, Bildarchiv Foto Marburg; p. 95 (left) Bodleian Library, (right) The Metropolitan Museum of Art, Bequest of George Blumenthal, 1941; p. 96, Scala; p. 97, Almasy; p. 98, Editorial Photocolor Archives (Museum of Catalan Art, Barcelona); pp. 98-99, Bulloz; p. 99 (top left) Bildarchiv Foto Marburg, (top right) Lauros-Giraudon, (bottom right) Scala; p. 100, Giraudon; p. 101, Sara Ames Wheeler; **Chapter 6** — p. 102, Weston Kemp; p. 104, Bodleian Library; p. 105, Courtesy of the Trustees of the British Museum; p. 106-107, Bodleian Library; p.108, Editorial Photocolor Archives; p. 110, The Frick Collection, New York City; p. 116, The Bettmann Archives; p. 119, Historical Pictures Service, Chicago; **Chapter 7** — p. 120, Carl E. Östman (R. Hermans); p. 122, Harrison Forman; p. 123, Carl E. Östman (R. Hermans); p. 128, Harrison Forman; p. 129, Magnum (Rene Burri); p. 131, Staatsbibliothek Berlin; p. 132, Courtesy of the Trustees of the British Museum; p. 134, Staatsbibliothek Berlin; p. 136 (both) Historical Pictures Service, Chicago; p. 138, Bodleian Library; **Chapter 8** — p. 140, Editorial Photocolor Archives; p. 142, Historical Pictures Service, Chicago; p. 143, Courtesy of the Trustees of the British Museum; p. 145, Courtesy of the Museum of Fine Arts, Boston; p. 147 (left) National Gallery of Art, Washington, D.C., (right) Courtesy of the Museum of Fine Arts, Boston, Bequest of Mrs. Thomas O. Richardson, (bottom) Courtesy of the Museum of Fine Arts, Boston, Gift of Quincy Adams Shaw; p. 150 (top left) Alan Band Associates, (lower left) De Wys, Inc., (lower right) Almasy; p. 151, Italian Government Tourist Office; p. 153, Historical Pictures Service, Chicago; p. 154, Alan Band Associates; p. 157, Giraudon; **Conclusion** — p. 158, Weston Kemp; p. 162 (top left) Editorial Photocolor Archives, (top right) Jewish Theological Seminary of America, (bottom) Scala; p. 163, Harrison Forman.

Illustrations and Charts: Laszlo Gal, pp. 34 and 126; Leslie Morrill, pp. 57, 71, 72, 80, 82; Diane Nelson, pp. 2, 4, 5, 39, 77, 88, 111, 114, 144, 148.

Map design and compilation by Allyn and Bacon.

A NOTE TO STUDENTS

To help you find out things for yourself and to use the things you know, think about the problems and questions as you read. They are marked ►, ●, or ★.

These symbols mean:

►   easy to solve
●   harder to solve — more thinking is needed
★   something extra — usually requires research

Many words in this book are respelled to help you pronounce them. The key below will help you read the respellings.

a	hat, cap	j	jam, enjoy	u	cup, butter
ā	age, face	k	kind, seek	u̇	full, put
ã	care, air	l	land, coal	ü	rule, move
ä	father, far	m	me, am	ū	use, music
		n	no, in		
b	bad, rob	ng	long, bring	v	very, save
ch	child, much			w	will, woman
d	did, red	o	hot, rock	y	young, yet
		ō	open, go	z	zero, breeze
e	let, best	ô	order, all	zh	measure, seizure
ē	equal, be	oi	oil, voice		
ėr	term, learn	ou	house, out	ə	represents:
					a in about
f	fat, if	p	paper, cup		e in taken
g	go, bag	r	run, try		i in April
h	he, how	s	say, yes		o in lemon
		sh	she, rush		u in circus
i	it, pin	t	tell, it		
ī	ice, five	th	thin, both		
		ŦH	then, smooth		

From THORNDIKE-BARNHART JUNIOR DICTIONARY by E. L. Thorndike and Clarence L. Barnhart. Copyright © 1968 by Scott, Foresman and Company.

Ebs
est
calõ
extī
ne
ac
cen
sus

in corde procedens ab
eo mediantibus spi
ritu i sanguine per
arterias. a uenas in
totum corp⁹ ￼Et

Jnflamatur meo mflamatioe
que nocet operatiombus natu
ralibus ￼Non sicut caloi
tas sic et calidus. Et cum non
ultimatur a impedit opeiti
onem ita ut itineat ￼Et
sunt quidam hominum qui
oiuidunt febrem moias a
oiuisiones pannas. s. in febres
egritudinem ain febrem ac
cidenē ￼Et pomunt febrem a
apostematum de grene febus
accidentis ￼Et i mtentio

Periods of History

The story of civilization is more than 5,000 years old. It is the story of many cultures in different parts of the world. Some of these cultures changed a great deal and became civilized. Some changed very little.

The story of these cultures is important to us because it is our story. To understand our own culture and civilization we must learn what has happened before our time. If we do not, we are like people who arrive late at a movie. They see just the last three minutes of the movie and try to understand what is going on.

Using a Time Line—Ancient Civilization

Before we continue our study of the Human Adventure, let us review the first 3,000 years. Those years form a pattern. One of the best ways to see that pattern is to use a time line.

A time line of ancient civilization is shown on page 2. Each year takes up very little space. This is because the time line must

TIME LINE OF ANCIENT CIVILIZATION

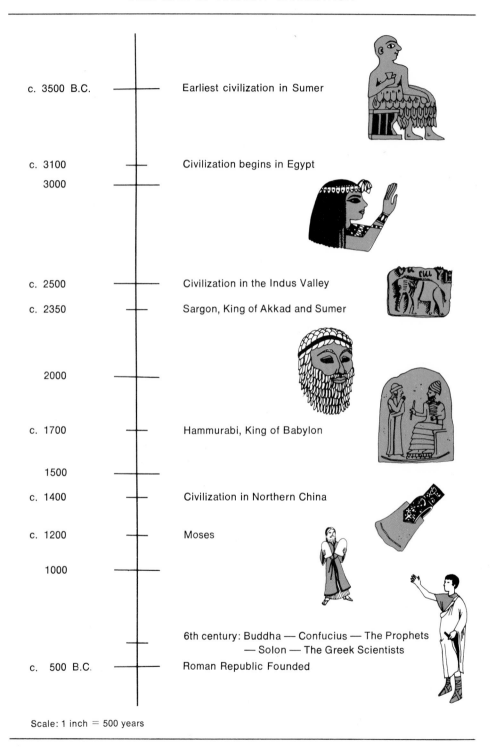

c. 3500 B.C. — Earliest civilization in Sumer

c. 3100 — Civilization begins in Egypt

3000 —

c. 2500 — Civilization in the Indus Valley

c. 2350 — Sargon, King of Akkad and Sumer

2000 —

c. 1700 — Hammurabi, King of Babylon

1500 —

c. 1400 — Civilization in Northern China

c. 1200 — Moses

1000 —

6th century: Buddha — Confucius — The Prophets — Solon — The Greek Scientists

c. 500 B.C. — Roman Republic Founded

Scale: 1 inch = 500 years

cover a long period. Most of the dates are not definite because they cover events that took place over many years. Some dates are not definite because the records are not definite. These records come to us from earlier times. Often, they do not give exact dates.

Some of the dates in the time line are used for a special purpose. They help to show **trends**, or general developments. In front of these dates, we use the abbreviation "c.," which means "circa." *Circa* comes from a Latin word that means "about" or "around."

▶ Using the time line of ancient civilization answer the following questions:

How many years does the time line cover? How many years does one inch of the time line stand for?

When did the first civilization arise? Where was it? Where were the next two civilizations?

When did the controlling ideas of Confucianism, Buddhism, Judaism, and Greek "naturalism" develop?

The Time Line of Classical, or Greco-Roman, Civilization

We sometimes call the period of the Greek city-states and of Rome **classical civilization**. The main period of classical civilization began about 500 B.C. It lasted until about A.D. 500. You can see this on the time line on pages 4-5. The scale here is different from the scale for the time line of ancient civilization. Compare the two scales. Why are they different? Because the time line of classical civilization covers only 1,000 years—not 3,000. Classical civilization did not last as long as ancient civilization. Therefore, more space can be used for each year on the time line of classical civilization.

Before classical civilization began, there were many different civilizations in the world. We have studied some of them.

▶ Look at a world map and note the many places where there were civilizations before classical civilization began.

TIME LINE OF CLASSICAL CIVILIZATION   500 B.C.—1 B.C.

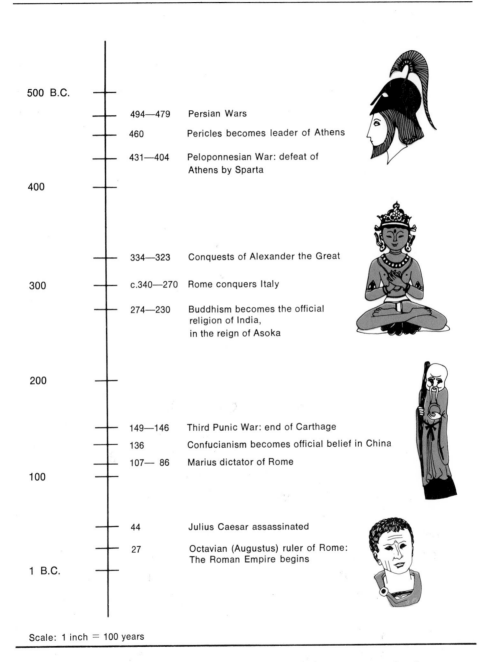

500 B.C.		
	494—479	Persian Wars
	460	Pericles becomes leader of Athens
	431—404	Peloponnesian War: defeat of Athens by Sparta
400		
	334—323	Conquests of Alexander the Great
300	c.340—270	Rome conquers Italy
	274—230	Buddhism becomes the official religion of India, in the reign of Asoka
200		
	149—146	Third Punic War: end of Carthage
	136	Confucianism becomes official belief in China
	107— 86	Marius dictator of Rome
100		
	44	Julius Caesar assassinated
	27	Octavian (Augustus) ruler of Rome: The Roman Empire begins
1 B.C.		

Scale: 1 inch = 100 years

Classical civilization was important because it had a great influence on our own civilization. However, during this time, other civilizations were also ebbing and flowing. They were

TIME LINE OF CLASSICAL CIVILIZATION   A.D. 1—A.D. 500

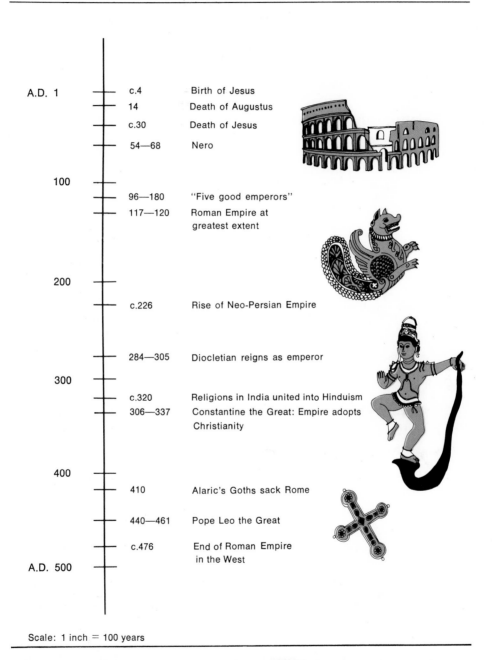

A.D. 1	c.4	Birth of Jesus
	14	Death of Augustus
	c.30	Death of Jesus
	54—68	Nero
100		
	96—180	"Five good emperors"
	117—120	Roman Empire at greatest extent
200		
	c.226	Rise of Neo-Persian Empire
	284—305	Diocletian reigns as emperor
300		
	c.320	Religions in India united into Hinduism
	306—337	Constantine the Great: Empire adopts Christianity
400		
	410	Alaric's Goths sack Rome
	440—461	Pope Leo the Great
	c.476	End of Roman Empire in the West
A.D. 500		

Scale: 1 inch = 100 years

ebbing and flowing in China, India, North Africa, and the Middle East. In China during this period, Confucianism became the official teaching. In India, Buddhism became an important religion.

Greek and Persian ideas were brought to India by Alexander the Great. There they mixed with ideas from Indian civilization. In the Middle East, another mixing took place. Greek culture mixed with Judaic and ancient Middle Eastern cultures. All these events took place during the time of classical civilization.

The Relationship Between Events

By looking at a time line, we can see two types of relationships between events. One of these relationships is *parallel.* The other is *sequential.* We will study each of these new words in turn.

Events that take place at about the same time, but in different cultures or societies, have a **parallel relationship.** Let us take an example. The time line of ancient civilization reminds us that Buddha and Confucius lived at about the same time. However, Buddha was part of Indian civilization, and Confucius was part of Chinese civilization.

- Look up the word *parallel* in your dictionary. Study the definitions. Why is this a good word to use to describe this relationship? Can you think of a better word? What?

Sequential means "following after." Events that take place at different times, but in the same culture or society, have a **sequential relationship.** In this kind of relationship, the earlier event does not always cause the later event. Usually, however, there is some connection between the two.

Here are some questions about parallel and sequential relationships. Use the time lines of ancient and classical civilizations to help you answer them.

- How were the Persian Wars, the rise of Pericles and the Athenian Empire, and the Peloponnesian War connected with one another?

- Explain the sequential relationship between the end of the Roman Empire in the West and the sacking of Rome by the barbarian Goths.

- What was the sequential relationship between Alexander and Hellenistic culture?

- What was the sequential relationship between the political troubles in the Roman Republic (the rise of military dictators like Marius and Julius Caesar) and the establishment of Roman power in the Mediterranean?

What Is an Historical Period?

The age of classical civilization was followed by what we call "the Middle Ages," or "the medieval (mē' dē ē' vl) period." **Medieval** comes from Latin words meaning "of the Middle Ages." The Middle Ages lasted from about A.D. 500 to about 1500.

Classical civilization, or the Classical Age, and the Middle Ages are historical periods. **Historical periods** are simply divisions of time that help us to keep track of history. They are not rigid and clear-cut. A Roman man living in A.D. 500 did not wake up on New Year's morning in 501 and say: "Goodbye, Classical Age! A Happy Middle Ages to all!" In fact, it was not until after 1500 that anyone called this period the Middle Ages.

The men who first called this period the Middle Ages were historians in Western Europe. They thought that the time between A.D. 500 and 1500 had been confused and uncivilized. It was a time between two great periods—the Classical Age—and their own time. Anything in between was "in the middle" so they called it the Middle Ages.

- We divided the earlier parts of *The Human Adventure* into ancient and classical civilization. Do you think these parts could be divided differently? Into more than two periods? Give some examples.

- Why is it helpful to use the end of the Roman Empire in the West as a dividing point between two periods?

- Why is it a mistake to choose a single date to mark a gradual change in history? When did the Roman Empire in the West begin to decline? When did the great Classical Age come to an end?

- In this book, you are going to read about the great Arab civilization. It was at its height from the middle of the eighth century to the thirteenth century. Do you think Arab historians would call this period the Middle Ages? Why or why not?

How Close Are We to the Middle Ages?

In some ways, the Middle Ages seem close to us. As we shall see in this book, the people of Western Europe built a new civilization during the Middle Ages. Today there is hardly any part of the world that is not influenced by the civilization they built. It is this influence that makes the Middle Ages seem close to us.

In actual time, the Middle Ages *are* quite close to us. There is one way to see how close they are. Let us count the generations (jen'ər ā'shənz) that separate us from our medieval ancestors. A **generation** includes all of the people who are born at about the same time. You and your friends and your brothers and sisters are all in one generation. Your parents and their friends are in the generation that came just before your generation. Your grandparents are in the generation that came just before your parents' generation.

How many years does a generation include? Most people have children when they are between 20 and 40 years old. The average age for people to become parents is about 30 years old. So the average length of time for measuring a generation is 30 years.

- Find out how old your parents were when you and your brothers and sisters were born. Find out how old your grandparents were when your parents and aunts and uncles were born. Do you think 30 years is a good length of time for measuring the difference between generations?

- Counting 30 years as a generation, how many generations have there been in your family since 1500? How many generations have there been in your family since 1000?

If you counted correctly, you discovered that your family has had only about 15 generations since the Middle Ages. That makes the Middle Ages seem close, doesn't it?

A Time of Violent Change—Medieval Civilization

We have said that the Middle Ages seem close to us in influence and in time. In other ways, however, they seem far removed from

The barbarian craftsmen produced not only weapons, but some very beautiful jewelry. This seventh-century pin was created with gold, bits of blue glass, and semiprecious stones.

us. The way of life during the Middle Ages seems far removed from our way of life. By A.D. 500, barbarians were sweeping over most of Europe, Asia, and North Africa. They brought with them a time of violent change. Their invasions upset most of the civilized world.

During the Middle Ages, barbarians attacked civilized lands from Western Europe to the borders of China. Their attacks were usually successful. Many barbarians fought on horseback. They lived off the land and moved swiftly. They fought against armies that carried many supplies and moved slowly. Such civilized armies were no match for the fast-moving barbarian horsemen.

Throughout the civilized world, the barbarians caused disorder and suffering. Out of all this disorder came changes in civilization. The first change was the result of a new religion. Let us see how this religion arose and gave rise to a new civilization.

► What does the word *barbarian* mean?

chapter 1

The Rise of Islam

Islam (is'ləm) is one of the world's largest religions. It began in Arabia around A.D. 613. It started with the teachings of an Arab named Muhammad (mủ ham' əd). Islam became a new religion and a new way of life for the Arabian people at that time. They wanted to spread the message of Islam. They went to war to do it. The Arabs conquered lands that had not been united for 700 years. Today the great Islamic Empire is gone. However, there are still more than 490 million Muslims (muz' limz), or followers of Islam, in the world.

In this chapter we will study the land where Islam began. We will study the people who developed this civilization. In particular, we will study the man who founded this religion.

- Look at the map on page 12 showing the Muslim world of today. In what parts of the world is Islam practiced?

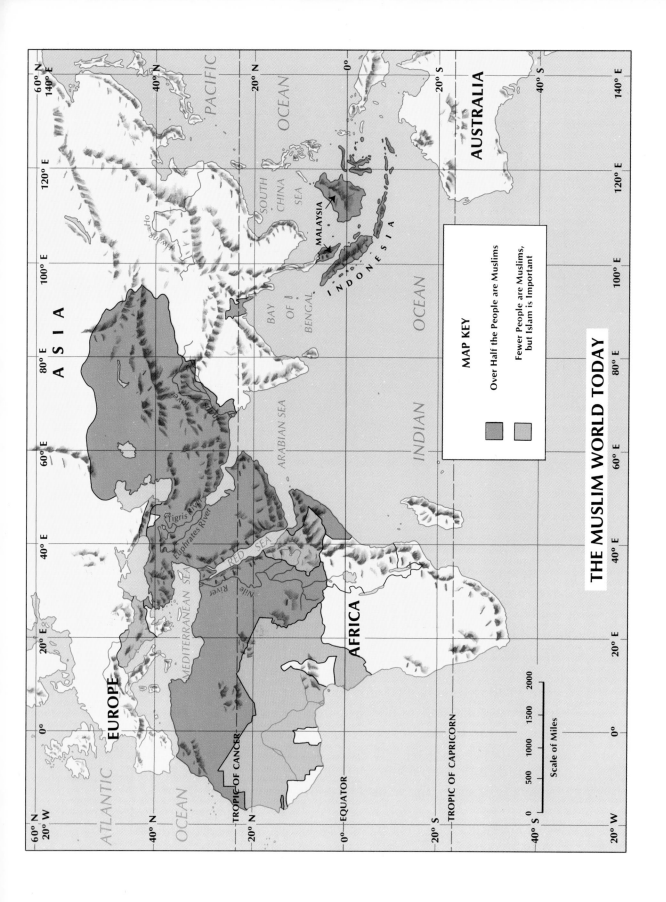

THE MUSLIM WORLD TODAY

MAP KEY

Over Half the People are Muslims

Fewer People are Muslims, but Islam is Important

The Land of the Desert

Arabia is a hot land. Most of it is desert, where the sun shines day after day. During part of the year, the temperature can rise to 120 degrees.

Arabia is also a dry land. Sometimes years pass without a drop of rain. Arabia was not always this dry. This land is cut by many **wadis** (wä' dēz), or dry river beds. Once they were great rivers. Today, water flows in them only after rain. Most of the time, the Arabs can use the wadis as roads for crossing the desert.

In the northern part of the Arabian Peninsula, hot winds sweep across rocky ground. The desert surface is stones and pebbles. There are a few thin patches of grass. Farther south, the desert is sandy. The winds blow the sand into hills that look like huge waves. These hills of sand are called sand dunes. Some sand dunes may be piled as high as 700 feet. During storms, the sand is blown into the air. People caught in sandstorms can hardly see or breathe. Whole armies have been lost and buried beneath the sand.

- Find Arabia on the globe. Trace the lines of longitude that go through it. Trace the lines of latitude that go through it.

- What does the word *peninsula* mean? Look at the map on page 15 that shows rainfall in the Arabian Peninsula. Why is Arabia called a peninsula?

- Using the map again, find the desert regions of Arabia. Is most of the Arabian Peninsula desert land? Explain.

- Would you describe a rainy Saturday as good or bad weather? Do you think a desert Arab would describe it in the same way? Explain.

The People of the Desert

For most of us, the Arabian desert would not make a good home. Still, some people manage to live there. These people are called Bedouin (bed' ů in). The **Bedouin** are nomads, or "people of the tent." They are tough, strong people who must continually move

These Bedouin nomads and their camels are very much at home in the desert. They know how to live with the sandstorms which can turn a welcome oasis (below, left) into a howling wasteland (below, right).

from place to place. They always take their camels, sheep, or goats with them.

● What do you think the Bedouin are looking for? What do they need for themselves? For their animals?

The animals provide most of the things the Bedouin need. They provide milk and cheese for food. The Bedouin live in tents made of camel or goat hair. For clothing, they use camel hair and wool.

Not all Arabs are nomads. Some have settled in certain parts of the desert. The desert has a few oases (ō ā′ sēz). **Oases** are fertile places where there is always a water supply. One such place is called an **oasis**. In an oasis, people can settle down, grow food,

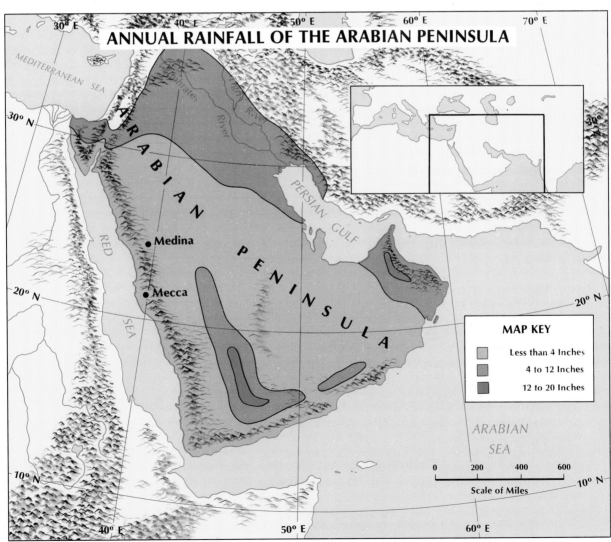

ANNUAL RAINFALL OF THE ARABIAN PENINSULA

MAP KEY

Less than 4 Inches

4 to 12 Inches

12 to 20 Inches

and build towns. Merchants who are crossing the desert stop at oases to rest and trade.

In parts of Arabia there is enough rainfall for farming. Here farmers grow grain and sweet-smelling spices. The farmers may send their products away by caravan (kar′ ə van). A **caravan** is a group of people who travel together across the desert. They use camels to carry themselves and their goods. Around A.D. 600, caravans carried goods for merchants. They carried ivory from Africa, rubies from India, and silk from China. The merchants sold these things in Persia or Egypt or Syria. While crossing the desert, the caravans stopped at oases. That is how some oasis towns became rich. The most important of these towns was Mecca.

● Why would the caravans help oasis towns to grow rich?

The Early Life of Muhammad

Muhammad was born in Mecca in A.D. 570. At the time of his birth, the Arabs believed in a chief god named Allah (al′ ə). However, they did not think that Allah was the only god. The Arabs were polytheists. They believed there were many gods. These gods lived mostly in trees or wells or springs. The most powerful gods lived in stones. The Arabs wanted to keep the powerful stone-gods happy.

Long before Muhammad was born, one stone-god had become especially important. This was the god of the black stone in

Mecca. The black stone was kept in a cube-shaped building called the Kaaba (kā' bə). Once each year, tribesmen from all over Arabia traveled to Mecca. They went to honor the stone-gods, and the god of the black stone in particular.

- Why would wells, trees, and big stones be especially important to the Arabs? Think about the land and climate in most of Arabia.

- Which usually developed first—a belief in one God or a belief in many gods?

The Muslims say that a dazzling light shone in the sky when Muhammad was born. They tell many stories about strange events in Muhammad's childhood. Let us read two of them.

A VISIT FROM TWO ANGELS

One day, when Muhammad was four years old, he was tending sheep. Suddenly, two angels flew down. They grabbed the boy and laid him on the ground. Then they opened his stomach. From his heart they plucked out a black drop. Then they washed him with snow. All evil was thus washed away from Muhammad. From that time on, everyone knew that he would do great things.

A MONK GIVES A FEAST

When Muhammad was only 12 years old, he traveled to Syria with a caravan. For weeks the caravan had been moving over dusty desert trails. The animals, traders, and slaves were ready for a rest.

Soon the caravan was to pass the house of a Christian monk known for his wisdom. No one expected help from this holy monk. He had never before paid any attention to thirsty Arabs. As the caravan passed the monk's house, he called out to it. "Stop!" he said, "I want to entertain your caravan. Please be my guests at a great feast." He even invited the slaves and children. Imagine the merchants' surprise!

Young Muhammad received a special invitation. The monk said that he had seen a strange thing as Muhammad rode by. A tree had lowered its branches! The monk wanted to question the boy.

The monk was amazed when Muhammad answered his questions correctly. Then he examined Muhammad's body. Between the boy's shoulders he found the mark of a prophet. The monk promised that the boy would do very special things.

These stories about Muhammad are *legends*. They may be completely true, or only partly true. They may not be true at all!

● According to the New Testament, what unusual event occurred on the night of Christ's birth? Is this event similar to the story of Muhammad's birth?

Actually, few facts about Muhammad's early life are known. We do know that his family was well respected but not rich. By the time Muhammad was six years old, both his parents had died. An uncle took care of him while he grew up. When Muhammad was almost 25, his uncle gave him some advice. He said, "Muhammad, we do not have much money. I have heard that a rich widow is sending a caravan to Syria. Why don't you go to her and ask for work?"

The widow hired Muhammad. Later she offered to marry him. He accepted, and became leader of the caravan. Between trading trips, Muhammad had time to talk to many people. He especially liked to talk about religion with Jews and Christians who lived in Mecca. He heard many of their stories about prophets and angels. Most important, he heard about their faith in the one God. Muhammad began to think harder and harder about the one God. The harder he thought, the less he liked the stone-gods of the Arabs.

The Mission of Muhammad

When Muhammad was about 40 years old, he began to have strange dreams. He could not understand them. Visions appeared to him. He heard voices, but could not tell who had called to him. The Muslims believe that the Angel Gabriel appeared to Muhammad.

This is how Muhammad later described it: "The Angel Gabriel came to me while I was asleep. He was carrying a piece of silk cloth. On the cloth there was writing. He told me to read. I told him I could not read. Then, suddenly, the angel started to choke me so hard I thought I was going to die."

The same thing happened again. In the end, Muhammad found that he could read the angel's message. When he awoke, it was as though some words were written on his heart. The words were: "La ilāha illa-l-Lāh" — "There is no God but Allah." These words were also written: "Muhammadun rasūl-u-l-Lāh" — "Muhammad is Allah's Prophet." Muhammad spent the rest of his life preaching this message to the Arabs. He believed that Allah had chosen him to tell men what they should believe. That was his mission.

Muhammad began to preach this new message to his people in Mecca. He told the people that they were foolish to believe in many gods. They must surrender to Allah, the one true God. Muhammad told his people they must give up their careless ways of living. From Muhammad's message came the name of the new religion — Islam. Islam is the Arabic word for surrender or giving up.

Muhammad's followers then became known as Muslims. Muslim means one who surrenders. A Muslim is a person who surrenders his life and thoughts to the will of God. Since Muhammad based his message on the belief in one God, all Muslims are monotheists.

▶   What does *monotheist* mean?

▶   Name two other monotheistic religions.

Muhammad the Lawgiver

In the beginning, Muhammad did not intend to establish a new religion. He simply wanted the Arabs to give up their stone-gods. He wanted them to worship the one true God alone. For a while, the leaders of Mecca thought Muhammad was harmless. As he continued to preach, however, the Arab leaders turned against him. They did not like to be told they were foolish and ignorant. Mecca became a dangerous place for Muhammad and his followers.

In A.D. 622, Muhammad fled from Mecca. A close friend, Abu Bekr (ə bü bek'ər), went with him. The two men fled to an Arabian city called Medina. Their secret journey to Medina is called the **Hegira** (hi jī' rə). Hegira is the Arabic word for "departure." The Hegira marks the turning point in the history of Islam. In Medina, Muhammad could attract many more followers than he had before. There, Islam could develop into a new religion.

Along with the Arabs, there were many Jews and Christians living in Medina. Muhammad was glad to see them. He believed that God had spoken early in history. First, said Muhammad, God spoke through the Hebrew Prophets. Later, he said, God spoke through Jesus Christ. Now God's message was coming from the last and greatest of His Prophets. That, of course, was Muhammad himself. Muhammad thought that the Jews and Christians would be delighted to hear his message. After all, did they not worship the same God that he worshipped? To his surprise, Muhammad learned that the Jews and Christians did not like his message. They did not believe that he was the last of the Prophets.

In Medina, Muhammad founded his own community of believers. It was separate from the Christians and Jews. This Mus-

These pages from a handwritten copy of the Koran date from the thirteenth century.

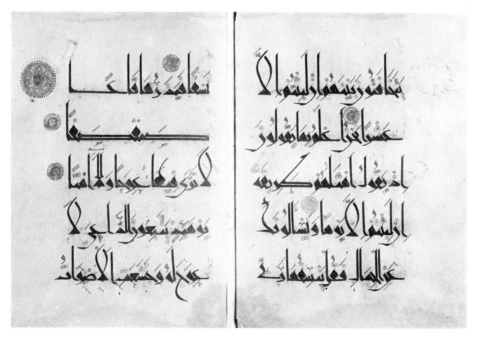

lim community presented many problems. Many of its members were farmers. They needed land for planting their crops. They also needed laws to help them live together. They wanted laws that were based on the will of Allah.

Muhammad was head of the Muslim community. He had to become a political leader as well as a religious leader. His followers agreed to live by the messages that he received from Allah. They agreed to follow laws that were based on these messages. The laws controlled every part of a Muslim's life. Muhammad told the Muslims when to pray and when to *fast* or avoid eating. He made rules for marriage. He made rules for carrying on business.

▶ Were Muhammad's laws religious or political or both? Explain.

● Who was supposed to be the ruler of the Muslims—Muhammad or Allah? How did this make it harder to break the law?

● Did the Hebrew Prophets claim to be speaking for God? Did Confucius or Buddha?

● Muhammad's name is sometimes spelled "Mohammed." Muslim is sometimes spelled "Moslem." What might cause these differences in spelling?

After Muhammad's death, his important teachings were collected in the Koran (kô rän'). The **Koran** is the sacred book of Islam. Many people say that Islam is like a building resting upon five pillars. The pillars are five religious duties. Every Muslim must perform these duties. Muhammad wanted every Muslim to be able to obey these duties. He tried not to make them too difficult. The Koran tells what these five pillars are. Let us read about them.

The First Pillar of Islam—The Act of Faith

Every Muslim must say that he believes in Allah. He must also say that he believes in Allah's prophet, Muhammad. This is called making an act of faith. Every Muslim must also believe in the Koran. Notice that the Muslims do not worship Muhammad. They worship only Allah.

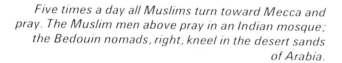

Five times a day all Muslims turn toward Mecca and pray. The Muslim men above pray in an Indian mosque; the Bedouin nomads, right, kneel in the desert sands of Arabia.

Muslims believe that Allah is close to men. As Allah says in the Koran, "I created man; and I know what his heart whispers to him, and I am closer to him than the vein in his neck."

Muhammad did not want a special group of priests to stand between Allah and Allah's people. He did not want anyone—even himself—to come between them. Muhammad insisted that he was only a man. He said that he was only trying to do the will of Allah. That, he said, was the highest purpose in life.

● Why does a Muslim not like to be called a Muhammadan?

The Second Pillar of Islam—Prayer

Five times a day, all Muslims are called to prayer. Five times a day, the same sound is heard in all Muslim lands. A man climbs the tower of a **mosque** (mosk), which is a Muslim place of worship. He sings out, "God is most great. I believe there is no god but Allah. I believe that Muhammad is the messenger of Allah. Come to prayer. Come to salvation. God is most great! There is no god but Allah."

Whatever a Muslim is doing then, he stops to pray. First he washes himself, no matter where he may be. If he is in the desert, he washes himself with sand. Then he kneels on his prayer rug, and turns toward Mecca to pray. Muhammad himself once said: "The comfort of my heart has been prayer."

The Third Pillar of Islam—Giving to the Poor

Muhammad commanded the Muslims to help people in need. In the early days of Islam, Muslims had to pay a "loan to God." This meant giving alms to the Muslim community. **Alms** are money or animals or grain, given freely to help the poor. The Koran says: "Be good to the poor and to your neighbors, whether they are friends or strangers. Be good to fellow-travelers and to slaves."

- What other religious leaders have taught men to be kind and merciful?

- How might giving alms help to unite all Muslims as brothers?

The Fourth Pillar of Islam—Fasting

Fasting is also important to the Muslims. The Koran says that Muslims should give up some food and drink to help them fight off evil. For one month each year, Muslims cannot eat, drink, or smoke from sunrise until sunset. They call this month **Ramadan** (ram' ə dän').

Ramadan is more than a time of fasting. It is also a time of prayer. At the end of Ramadan, Muslims celebrate with a great party. They feast on dried fruit, sweet buns, and little pancakes dipped in powdered sugar.

- Do Christians and Jews have periods of fasting? Explain.

- Do you think fasting is important to religion? What connection can there be between worshipping God and fasting?

The Fifth Pillar of Islam—The Pilgrimage to Mecca

At least once before they die, Muslims must try to go to Mecca. They must try to visit the Kaaba there. As we have seen, the Kaaba was once the home of one of the stone-gods. Muslims believe that the one true God commanded Abraham to build the Kaaba. They believe that the black stone was given to Abraham by the Angel Gabriel. The Hebrews called Abraham the founder of Judaism.

- Why do you think the Muslims would honor Abraham as a great prophet? (Consider: What was Abraham's message to the Hebrews?)

In Mecca today, one can often see great crowds of pilgrims. They are obeying the command in the Koran: "Proclaim to the peoples a pilgrimage. Let them come on foot and on camel. Let them arrive in deep lines." The pilgrims gather in a large tiled courtyard. The men are all dressed alike, in plain white robes. That shows that all men are equal before Allah. The pilgrims circle about the Kaaba. Many of them go up to the black stone set in the wall of the Kaaba. They kiss the stone to show that they believe in Allah.

- Did Arabs before the time of Muhammad make a pilgrimage to Mecca? Why?

- Did Muhammad continue to use a tradition of the past? Do you think this was wise? Did Muhammad make any changes in the tradition?

What Muhammad Taught About the Brotherhood of Faith

As Muhammad preached, more and more Arabs became Muslims. They agreed to live by the laws that Muhammad laid down for them. Soon Muhammad was faced with a new problem. He had to find some way of holding all his followers together. How could he do this?

The Arabs were divided into many different tribes. Often these tribes hated one another. Muhammad had come to Medina in the first place because of a fight between two tribes. The leaders of these tribes heard of Muhammad's wisdom and honesty. They asked him to come and make peace. Muhammad did so. Several years later, he wanted to make peace between all Arabs.

An Arab was fiercely loyal to the tribe of his birth. In defense of a relative, he would gladly kill or be killed. Muhammad wanted the Arabs to keep their feelings of tribal loyalty. However, their faith in God must come first, he said.

Muhammad said that all Muslims must unite to form one people. All Muslims must be brothers. That, he said, was the will of Allah. Muslims must not fight among themselves. Their reli-

Muslim pilgrims circle the Kaaba in Mecca. Each year thousands of faithful Muslims travel to this sacred place.

gious belief must become stronger than anything else. Muhammad replaced "blood brotherhood" with the "brotherhood of faith." In years to come, the brotherhood of faith came to include huge numbers of people. It included millions who were not Arabs.

▶ How did Muhammad change the old Arab idea of loyalty?

● Which group would include more people—Arabs united by faith in Allah or Arabs united by membership in a certain tribe? Explain.

What Muhammad Taught About "Holy War"

One of the most important Muslim teachings probably goes back to Muhammad's early years in Medina. At that time, he was just learning that the Jews and Christians would not accept his message. They were laughing at the idea that he could be a prophet. The Muslim community had too little land and food. Its members were beginning to grow hungry. Back in Mecca, the rich merchants heard about Muhammad's bad luck. They said it was a sign that Allah was angry with him.

This may have been when Muhammad got the idea of a "holy war." To get the things his followers needed, he sent out a few men to raid a caravan from Mecca. This was the first of the Muslims' many battles against "enemies of Allah." Such battles did two things. They proved the power of Allah, and they brought in rich treasure.

The Muslims soon learned they could get what they needed by fighting. Some of Muhammad's followers were eager to fight because of their faith in Allah. Some were eager to fight because they wanted booty. **Booty** means all the things that a fighter takes from defeated enemies. Muhammad's success in battle convinced many Arabs that he was a true prophet. To them, his victories proved that Allah was on his side. They could see that it would be profitable to join him.

By the time Muhammad died, most of Arabia had become Muslim. The idea of a "holy war" had become part of Islam. Muhammad promised that Allah's soldiers would win an even greater reward in Paradise.

"You are commanded by God to fight, even though you may not like it."

"God has promised you much booty. And you shall have it."

"Do not think that those killed on God's battlefield are dead. No! They are alive with their Lord."

● How did the holy war help to strengthen religion as the bond uniting the Arabs?

● In what ways did Muhammad make war attractive to his followers?

The Third Great Monotheistic Religion

Muhammad died in A.D. 632. During his lifetime, he made very deep changes in the lives and beliefs of the Arabs. As Muslims, they gave up their separate tribal gods. In accepting Muhammad's message, they became one people. Their unity of belief brought them political unity. They obeyed one God — Allah. They obeyed one leader — Muhammad.

Islam became the world's third great monotheistic religion. Yet in many ways it was quite similar to Judaism and Christianity. It still is. Many people forget this. They think only about the things that make the three religions different from one another. Let us review what we have learned about Islam by relating it to Judaism and Christianity.

▶ Are Christianity, Judaism, and Islam monotheistic? Explain.

● In what part of the world did Judaism begin? In what part did Christianity and Islam begin?

● Do Christians, Jews, and Muslims believe people should submit their lives to God? Explain.

● Do Christians, Jews, and Muslims believe in good works, prayer, and fasting? Explain.

● Do you think that many of the goals of Islam are the same as goals of Judaism and Christianity? How do you think the three religions are different?

This Muslim manuscript illustrates the story of Noah's ark.

chapter 2

The Spread of Islam

Long before Muhammad's time, the Arabs knew about their more civilized neighbors. They knew that these neighbors had wealth. The Arabs wanted to share in this wealth. As Muslims, they learned how they could share in it—through conquest.

Once the Muslims were united, they could conquer lands that were highly civilized. They did not destroy these civilizations. Instead, they began to learn from them. The Muslims began to change from the ways of the desert to the ways of civilized men.

In conquering new lands, the Muslims learned new ideas. They learned about science from ancient Greece. They learned about mathematics from India. They learned about architecture from Syria, Persia, and Egypt. Then they began to make experiments of their own. They began to mix their own ideas with the ideas of other peoples. In so doing, they created a new culture in a new civilization.

- What do you know about other peoples who lived on the edges of civilization and wanted to share in the wealth of civilization?

- Can you give any other examples of conquerors who borrowed ideas from the people they conquered?

In this chapter, we shall see what happened to Islam after the death of Muhammad. We will study the new civilization that arose in the Arab lands. This civilization was brilliant and powerful. As you read about it, keep these questions in mind.

What did religion have to do with Muslim art? Architecture? Philosophy?

What did Islamic culture gain from the conquered peoples?

The First Caliph

Muhammad believed that he had been chosen to speak for Allah. When Muhammad died, he left no one to take his place. Islam might have died with him—but it did not. The Arabs went through bitter political struggles. Still, the teachings of Muhammad continued to unite Islam. How was this possible?

After Muhammad died, some of the older Muslims met. They chose a new leader, called the **caliph** (kā' lif). The caliph was Muhammad's successor. However, the caliph was only a ruler. He was not a prophet. After all, Muhammad had said that *he* was the last of the prophets.

For first caliph, the Muslims chose Abu Bekr. Since the early days in Mecca, Abu Bekr had been Muhammad's close friend. In fact, one of Muhammad's wives had been Abu Bekr's daughter. Abu Bekr did not look like a great leader. He was short and walked with a stoop. Yet he proved to be a great caliph.

Almost at once, Abu Bekr had a chance to prove himself. Trouble was coming. Some tribes refused to follow him as caliph. They said they had promised loyalty only to Muhammad. Now that he was dead, why should they obey anyone else? Other tribes had never accepted Islam in the first place. Now they hoped to destroy the power of the Muslims. Civil war broke out in Arabia. In the end, the war was won by the Muslim forces under Abu Bekr. Then, with peace at home, Islam went on the march. Instead of fighting among themselves, the Arabs could start fighting other peoples.

Islam on the March

The Muslims soon defeated the two empires that bordered Arabia. These were the Persian Empire and the Byzantine Empire. The Persian Empire lay to the north of Arabia. The Byzantine territory lay to the northwest. For many years, these two empires had been at war with each other. In earlier times they had been mighty. Now, however, war had left them weak and tired.

The Muslims did not plan to build a mighty empire of their own. They simply wanted to share in the wealth of their neighbors. Their way of sharing was to take what they could. They began by attacking a few Byzantine towns. To their surprise, they found that the Byzantines were weak and easily conquered. The Muslims soon began to move over wider areas. Why shouldn't they attack civilized societies! They had nothing to lose. If they lived, they would gain great treasure. If they died, they would go straight to Paradise.

In their fighting, the Arabs did not rely on any special weapons. Their greatest weapon was their knowledge of the desert. The Arabs knew how to travel and live on the desert better than their enemies. Here is the advice one Arab general gave to his men.

> Fight the enemy in the desert. Even if you lose, you will
> have the familiar desert at your backs. The enemy can-
> not follow you there. And from there you can return
> again to the attack.

The Muslims were filled with faith in Allah and faith in their own swords. They swept across the Middle East. Each new victory made them stronger. Their conquests became an all-out holy war for Allah. Their battle cry was, "Allah is most great." People soon learned that it was wise to surrender to the Arabs without fighting. If they surrendered, they would only have to pay the Arabs a tax. If they fought, the Arabs would probably defeat them and take their lands.

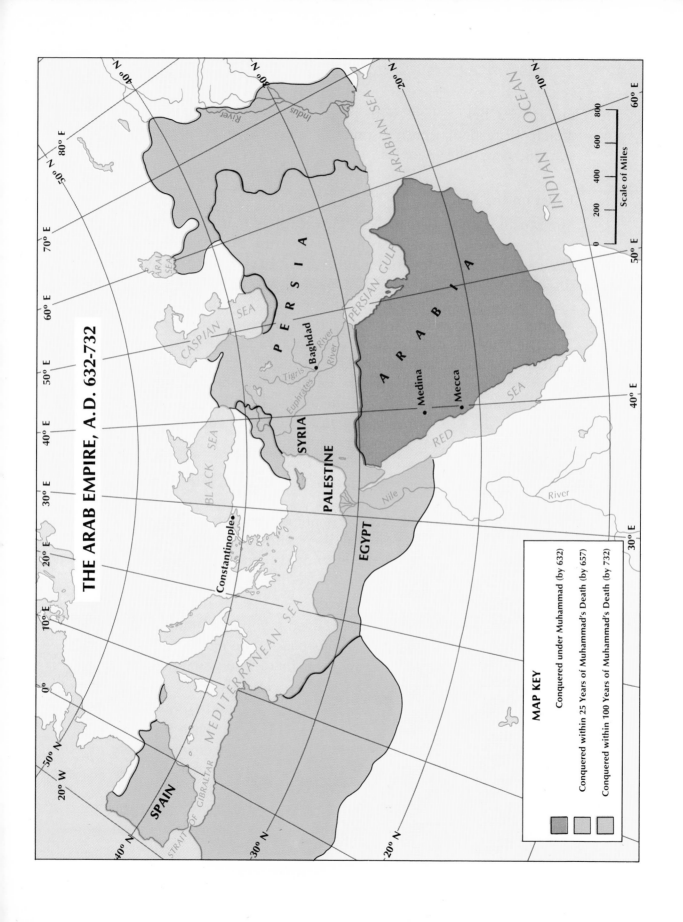

THE ARAB EMPIRE, A.D. 632-732

MAP KEY

Conquered under Muhammad (by 632)

Conquered within 25 Years of Muhammad's Death (by 657)

Conquered within 100 Years of Muhammad's Death (by 732)

Scale of Miles

0   200   400   600   800

INDIAN OCEAN

ARABIAN SEA

PERSIAN GULF

ARABIA

PERSIA

Baghdad

Tigris River

Euphrates River

Medina

Mecca

RED SEA

SYRIA

PALESTINE

EGYPT

Nile River

CASPIAN SEA

ARAL SEA

Indus River

BLACK SEA

Constantinople

MEDITERRANEAN SEA

SPAIN

STRAIT OF GIBRALTAR

River

The Muslims' control over other lands spread like a brush fire. Within one century after Muhammad's death, they controlled Egypt, Persia, North Africa, most of Spain, and part of India. When one Muslim general reached the Atlantic, he was sorry. He cried to Allah. "If this sea were not stopping me, I would go to the unknown kingdoms of the West, conquering all nations who worship other gods than Thee!"

- Look at the map on page 32 showing the Arab Empire. Had this whole area ever been included in one empire before?

- Compare the map of the Arab Empire with the map of the Muslim world of today on page 12. Which of the areas that were once controlled by the Arabs are still mainly Muslim today?

How the Caliphs Ruled the Empire

The Muslims did not have an easy time choosing caliphs to follow Abu Bekr. Different groups wanted different men to be caliphs. Muhammad and Abu Bekr had died naturally. Three out of the next four caliphs were murdered!

The early caliphs were chosen for more than their leadership. They were chosen for their holiness, too. They were more concerned with religion than with politics. The second caliph, for example, was very strict. Many Muslims feared him. Muhammad himself had once told this man, "If the Devil himself saw you coming down the street, he would dodge into a side alley."

As time went on, the caliphs began to worry more about politics and less about religion. They had to. They now had gained the problems of ruling an empire. Muslim law was still based on the Koran. It was still based on the example that had been set by Muhammad. Power, however, belonged to the caliph. Later caliphs became dictators. They used power as they pleased. These caliphs believed they were more than Muhammad's successors. They believed they were the "Shadows of God on Earth."

Here is a story about one caliph. It will give you an idea of how much power he had. Notice that he is called a king. This story is from *The Tales of a Thousand Nights and a Night*. This is a famous collection of stories often called *The Arabian Nights*.

THE STORY OF QUEEN SCHEHEREZADE

In the name of Allah, the Compassionate, the Merciful, Creator of the Universe, Who has raised the Earth without Pillars . . .

Long, long ago there lived a king who was married to a queen as beautiful as the sunrise. The king and queen loved each other very much—or so the king thought. But one day he discovered that the queen's sweet smiles hid a heart full of poison. She was plotting to murder him and marry another man. When the king found out the truth, he was so angry that he killed the queen. Not only that, he took a vow to marry many times. And he vowed that, on the morning after each wedding, he would cut off the head of his new bride!

So it happened that many young girls lost their heads in this way. Finally, there were no pretty women left in the kingdom. All the pretty women who were left alive had been sent away to a healthier climate. The only ones left were the two daughters of the king's chief official, the Grand Vizier (vi zir'). He had kept them at home, for he could not bear to part with them.

One day the king called for his Grand Vizier. "I have decided to marry again," he said. "Find me a wife."

"But Master, all the young maidens have fled from your kingdom!" cried the Grand Vizier. "There are no wives to be found."

The king replied, "If I do not have a bride by nightfall—off with your head!"

What was the poor old man to do? Sadly, he walked home.

The Grand Vizier's older daughter was named Scheherezade (shə hãr'ə zäd'). She was a girl as bright as she was beautiful. She had studied and thought very deeply. She knew a thousand different stories. When Scheherezade saw her father's long face, she guessed what the trouble was. "Do not worry, Father," she said. "I will marry the king. There is just one favor you can do. Early tomorrow morning, before the sun rises, send my sister to the palace. Tell her to bring us some sherbet cooled in snow. Then have her beg me to tell a story. Only make sure that she does not fail to come."

Scheherezade married the king. She was dressed in golden cloth scattered with jewels. A silken veil covered her hair. She looked lovelier than a garden in springtime. Everyone wept to think what would happen the following morning.

Early next day, Scheherezade's sister crept through the streets. She entered the palace, and came to the royal chamber.

"I have brought you some refreshment, O King. But to help pass the time until sunrise, please have my sister tell us a story."

"That is a good idea," replied the king. "Will you entertain us, Scheherezade?" So Scheherezade began to tell a story. She finished it and was all ready to start on a new story, when the sun came up.

"O, My Lord, I am sorry," she said. "This new story is even better than the first—but it is too late to begin it this morning."

The king answered, "Never mind. We will hear that story tomorrow."

That is how Scheherezade managed to live past the first night, and 999 nights after. Sometimes she would promise an even better story to come, or would mix up two or three different stories—not finishing any of them.

On the thousand and first night, Scheherezade did something she had never done before. She did not leave enough time before sunrise to start a new story. Instead, she turned to the king:

"O King, for a thousand nights I have told stories to entertain you. Everyone knows that you reward even one simple joke with great treasures—yet I have never asked for any reward. Now I would like to claim mine. Allah does not ask you to fulfill an evil vow. Give up your wicked promise—and tell our poor father that both my sister and I will be safe."

"Scheherezade, my Queen," answered the king, "I have known for a long time now that I would never be able to fulfill my vow. I have seen how lucky I am to have such a good wife. And I have grown to love you very much. This day, everyone in my kingdom will know that, too."

So the king and queen lived happily together forever after.

- What does this story tell you about the power of the Muslim rulers? About the place of women?

The caliphs' way of using power never changed. They used power as they pleased. Once, after a caliph had been killed, the new caliph gave a dinner. He invited 80 members of the dead caliph's family. During the dinner, he had all of them stabbed to death. He did not want any of them to live to challenge him.

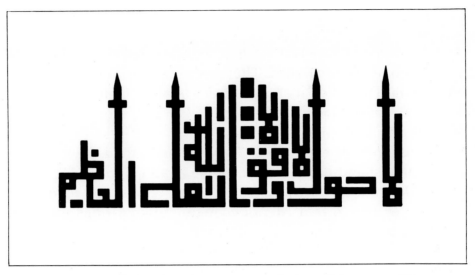

Arabs loved to use their written language to make beautiful patterns. This mosque-like design says "There is no strength and no power but that of the Almighty and All-powerful Allah."

The Arabic Language and the Muslim Faith

The Arabs did not have a long tradition of science and mathematics. They knew little of architecture and art. However, they did have two great gifts. These gifts were their Arabic language and their Muslim faith. With them the Arabs enriched the culture of the lands they conquered.

The Arabs loved the sound of their language. They especially loved its deep, rich tones. The Arabs also loved to write in Arabic. Like the Chinese, they made handwriting a great art. Their writing became a lovely thing to see. They could work a passage from the Koran into a beautiful design.

Besides their language, the Arabs were proud of their faith. Islam belonged to them. They believed that it was a special gift to them from Allah. Many of the conquered peoples learned Arabic. Many of them became Muslims, too. That is why the meaning of the word *Arab* began to change. Originally, an Arab was a person born on the Arabian Peninsula. In time, however, an Arab was anyone who wrote in Arabic and was a Muslim. It did not matter where he had been born. It did not matter what his ancestors' language was.

The Birth of Arab Culture

As the power of the Arabs grew, they learned more about the wonders of ancient cultures. They took ideas from Greece, India, and Persia. They even took ideas from faraway China. The Arabs could no longer be called barbarians. The more the Arabs learned, the more they wanted to learn. They asked questions. They observed. They studied. They experimented. Out of their lively interest and hard work came the Arab culture.

To learn from foreign writings, the Arabs had to do one thing. They had to translate, or change, these writings into Arabic. They translated many Greek and Indian writings into Arabic. Arabic scholars were especially interested in the ideas of the ancient Greeks. Like the Greeks, the Arabs began to trust man's ability to think and reason. They wanted to find out more about man and his world.

By translating the writings, the Arabs were able to save many of the great ideas of the past. If they had not, some of these ideas might have been lost forever. Soon the Arabs began to add new ideas of their own. They remained loyal to their belief in Allah, but they began to study the world of nature.

- Do you think it is important to save the writings of the past? Does the learning of the past mean anything in your life? Explain.

- Do you think translating is difficult? What would you have to know in order to translate well?

Arab Mathematics and Science

The Arabs learned that the Hindus of India had a special set of numerals. They adopted these numerals as their own. Today we use Hindu-Arabic numerals. They came to us through the Arabs.

The Arabs also learned that the people of India used a little circle or dot. It was called a *sifr* (sif' r). **Sifr** means empty. This word is the basis of our word cipher (sī fer), or zero. The Arabs used the *sifr* "to keep the rows." In other words, they used the *sifr* as we use the zero. They used it as a placeholder. This was 250 years before the zero was used in Europe. With the help of the *sifr*, the Arabs developed **algebra** (al'jə brə). Algebra is one of the most important kinds of mathematics.

● Explain why the *sifr* was important. Look at the chart of Hindu and Hindu-Arabic numerals below. Explain how the *sifr* "kept the rows." Try to describe what arithmetic was like before men invented zero.

HINDU AND HINDU-ARABIC NUMERALS

In Hindu-Arabic numerals, what is the number shown in the box at right?

HINDU	?	?	?	?	?	
HINDU-ARABIC	1	2	3	4	5	
HINDU	?	?	?	?	?	
HINDU-ARABIC	6	7	8	9	0	

The Arabs also learned about **astronomy** (əs tron' ə mē), the study of the stars. They built many buildings and instruments for looking at the stars. From earlier thinkers, Arab scientists learned that the earth was round. This was 700 years before Columbus sailed west across the Atlantic!

In medicine, the Muslims knew about many things that we think are modern. They used surgery to fight such a disease as cancer. They had hospitals and even traveling clinics. Muslim doctors knew that disease was not the work of devils. They knew it had natural causes. To choose the spot for a new hospital in Baghdad, one Muslim doctor had a good idea. He hung pieces of raw meat in different parts of the city. Then he watched to see in which place the meat rotted last of all. That is where he built his hospital.

● Why did the Muslim doctor choose that place?

The Muslims were serious students of **alchemy** (al' kə mē). Alchemy was half magic and half science and philosophy. It led to modern chemistry. The Muslims tried hard to find a way of turning cheap metals, such as lead, into gold. They never found how to do it. However, they did learn about many chemicals that they used. They saw the importance of testing. They kept notes and drew conclusions from what they saw. Then they tested again.

▶ Can you think of reasons why alchemy might be important even though alchemists were never able to turn lead into gold?

● Were the methods of the alchemists anything like those used by scientists today? Explain.

▶ From what ancient people did the Muslims get the idea that men should study the natural world?

Arab Art and Architecture

For Muslims, religion was the most important part of their lives. We can see this in their art. When the Arab soldiers conquered Greek and Persian lands, they saw temples. The Arabs thought these temples were beautiful. They wanted their own mosques to be just as beautiful. Every mosque had to follow the basic design of Muhammad's house. Muhammad's house had been built next to an open space. That is why every mosque had to have an open courtyard.

The mosques were beautiful inside as well as outside. Craftsmen carved lovely designs on the walls. The floors were covered by beautiful carpets. These carpets were woven in rich, glowing colors. Lamps made of fine glass hung from the ceilings. The windows of some mosques were made of colored glass. The doors had delicate patterns carved on them.

Muhammad had taught that only Allah could create life. Any artist who drew living creatures was trying to act like Allah. That was sinful, Muhammad said. Because of Muhammad's teaching, no pictures or statues of living creatures were allowed in the mosques. On the walls and ceilings, Muslim artists made geometric designs or patterns. Many of these designs were based on the forms of leaves and stems. Sometimes the Arabs based designs on the letters of the Arabic alphabet.

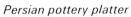

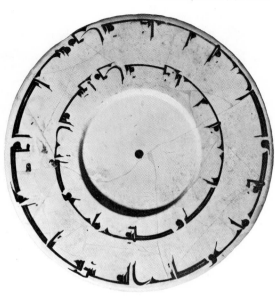

Arabic manuscript page

Arabs loved rich decoration and this love of design is evident in nearly everything they produced. Notice particularly the carving above the doorways in the open courtyard.

The Lion Fountain, The Alhambra, Spain

Notice the rich colors and design in this section of a magnificent Persian rug. Persia is as famous today for such rugs as it was in medieval times.

- What other reasons might Muhammad have for forbidding images? What do the Ten Commandments of Judaism and Christianity say about images?

- After learning about Muhammad's teachings, can you tell what Muslims would think of Christian art or Greek sculpture?

The Muslims made incense burners, lamps, jars, and swords that were beautiful as well as useful. They wove magnificent rugs. They designed colorful pottery. Rich Muslims copied the rich Persians by dressing in fine silks. Around their homes, the Muslims built gardens and fountains. They loved the sound of running water and the sight of bright colors reflected in pools.

- Why might the Arabs be especially fond of gardens and running water?

- The Arabs learned about many new things from the Persians. These things include mattresses, pillows, ovens, frying pans, and the game of chess. Which of them do we still use today?

- In A.D. 751, Arabs learned papermaking from captured Chinese workmen. What connection is there between the use of paper and the spread of knowledge?

The Economic Life of the Empire

Under Arab rule, trade grew in the Middle East. Arab merchants returned from India with spices and jewels. Caravans returned from China with precious silks and delicate porcelain. Ships returned from Africa with gold and ivory. These rare products were bought and sold in Arab markets. The markets were called **bazaars** (bə zärz′). The products of native Arab craftsmen were also sold in the bazaars.

There are still bazaars throughout the Muslim world. Here customers in Arabia bargain with cloth merchants.

- How did the location of the Arab Empire help the Arabs to build up trade with the East (China and India) and the West (Europe)?

- Could the people of Europe trade directly with China and India without going through Arab lands? Explain.

Cities like Baghdad and Damascus (də mas′kəs) became great trading centers. The roads leading to them were crowded with camel caravans. Port cities were crowded with merchant ships. Sea captains like Sinbad the Sailor roved the waterfronts.

★ Read and report on some of Sinbad's adventures in *The Arabian Nights*.

The Role of Slaves and Women

In the bazaars, human beings were also bought and sold. Arab traders bought slaves in Europe and Africa. They became rich by selling the slaves to wealthy men in the Muslim Empire.

As a rule, the slaves were not made to do only hard work. They were used mainly to make life easier and more pleasant for rich Arabs. Some were used as servants in homes. Some served in the Arab army.

- How were slaves used in ancient Greece and Rome? Which slaves would be most unhappy—those in Arab society or those in Greece and Rome? Explain.

Before Muhammad, the Arabs thought that women were weak and not as important as men. Baby girls were often killed. Little girls seven or eight years old could be married! Their fathers could give them to any man who paid the price they asked. Men could have as many wives as they wished. To the Arabs, wives were servants. Their first duty was to keep their husbands happy.

Muhammad made changes that helped Muslim women. He said that Muslims could not kill baby girls. He said that a man could not have more than four wives at once. To take four, he had to be able to support that many! Still, Muhammad felt that women were not as good as men. He said that a wife must obey her hus-

Although both these women in Algeria are still wearing veils, the little girl may be able to choose not to do so after she marries.

band in all things. The Koran ordered a husband to beat his wife if she did not obey him.

Many Muslim women began to cover their faces with veils. Only their fathers, husbands, and sons could see their faces. No other men could. This custom lasted in Muslim countries for many centuries after Muhammad's death. Some Muslim women still wear the veil.

Arab Culture Comes to Spain

Arab influence spread far beyond the Middle East. The Muslims ruled parts of Africa. They even ruled one part of Europe. That was Spain. The Muslims stayed in Spain for almost 800 years. During that time, Spain shared the rich Islamic culture. The university at Cordova (kôr′dō və) was one of the best in Europe.

Some Spanish Muslims studied and wrote about Greek philosophers. They tried to combine the Greek faith in man with their own faith in Allah.

The Arabs also helped Spain to become a great center of wealth. The Muslims brought orange trees and sugar cane to Spain. They taught the people new ways to irrigate the soil. They started some important industries. Among these were industries to produce steel, leather, paper, and cloth.

● Were the changes just described economic or political? Do you think the Arab invaders helped Spain or hurt it? Explain.

● What happened in Europe after the fall of the Roman Empire? Which do you think had the richer culture at this time — Muslim Spain or Christian Europe?

The Muslims brought many benefits to the Christians of Spain. Even so, the Spaniards hated them. They started a long fight to drive the Muslims out. In the end, the Spaniards won. Yet Muslim influence remained in Spain. From Spain, it passed to the rest of Europe. Because of the Arabs, Europe learned about many great ideas of the past.

● Why might Spanish Christians have wanted to drive the Muslims out of Spain?

● Is it true that the Arabs saved the great ideas of the Greeks for Europe? Explain your answer.

★ Which of the following things or ideas reached Europe because of the Arabs? Were all these things original inventions of the Arabs? Explain.

paper	patterns of decoration
translations of Greek works	automobiles
chemical methods	wares of skilled craftsmen
Hindu-Arabic numerals	control of disease
Christianity	the Old Testament
zero	the idea that men should study
polytheism	the natural world
Roman books and poems	Greek art

The Arab World Stops Growing

About the twelfth century A.D., the Arab Empire began to decline. Through the years, Muslim law did not change. The Muslims would not question Muhammad's commands. They would not question the way in which their scholars said they should obey those commands. The Arabs grew satisfied with their achievements. They did not care to learn new ideas. Slowly, the culture of Islam came to a standstill.

When the civilization of Islam was at its height, most of Europe was overrun by barbarians. Now the barbarians invaded Arab lands. In the end, most of the Arab Empire fell under the rule of the barbarians. These barbarians adopted the faith of the people they conquered. They became Muslims. Islam itself continued to grow, but the day of Arab leadership was over. The Arabs never again became as powerful as they had been.

- What often happens when a culture stands still?

- In what ways besides conquest can people learn from other people?

- Who are some other conquerors who adopted the faith of the people they conquered?

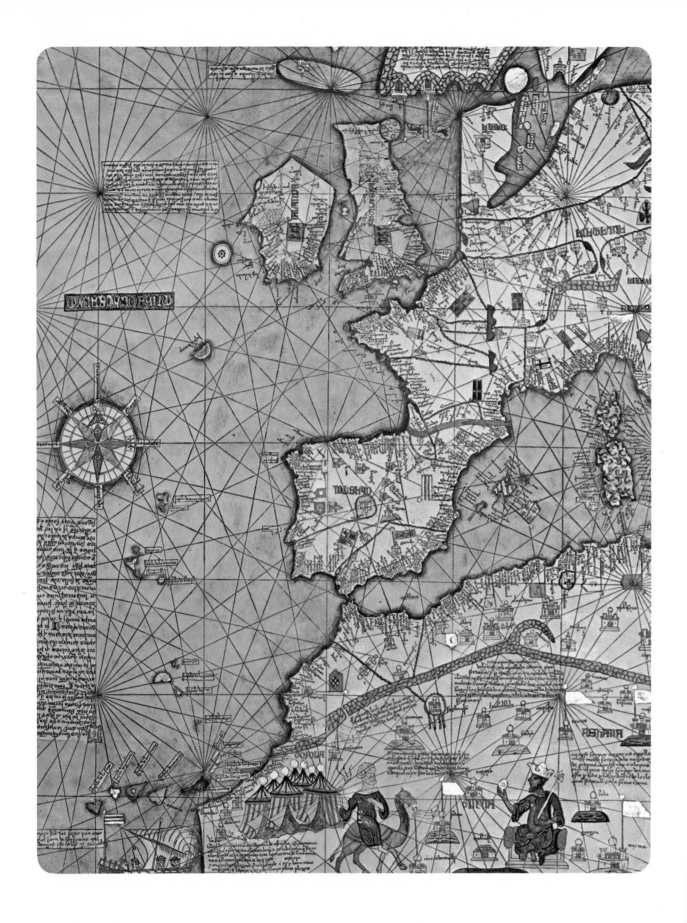

chapter 3

African Kingdoms

By the end of the seventh century, the Arabs had swept across North Africa. They had conquered the territory. They had converted most of the people to Islam. In A.D. 712, they were ready to attack Spain. Then they heard something that changed their plans. They heard about a land of great wealth—a "land of gold."

This land was the kingdom of Ghana (gä'nə) in Africa. It lay south of a great desert, the Sahara. The Arabs hoped to gain even greater wealth. They divided their armies in two. One army conquered Spain. The other army crossed the Sahara to find "the land of gold." To their amazement, they met a large and powerful black army. This army was even equipped with iron weapons! The Arabs retreated.

The Arab warriors failed, but the Arab merchants succeeded. The merchants came peacefully to trade their goods for Ghana's gold. They were welcomed. They proved that the reports of

Ghana's wealth were true. Their records tell us all we know about the early African kingdoms.

During the Middle Ages, there were three great kingdoms in Africa. These kingdoms arose one after the other. All three were located in a region just south of the Sahara. These kingdoms ruled the region from about A.D. 700 to 1600. They were called Ghana, Mali (mä'lē), and Songhai (sông'hī).

Ghana, Mali, and Songhai were rich and powerful trading centers. What produced them and their high level of civilization? The answer has many parts. Part of the answer is natural environment. Part of it is trade and surplus production. Strong political organization played an important part. So did the spread of Islam. Let us see how the different parts of the answer fit together.

Natural Environment of the Sudan

The region where Ghana, Mali, and Songhai arose is part of a large region called the **Sudan**. The Sudan stretches from west to east across Africa south of the Sahara. Its natural vegetation is mainly **savanna**, that is, dry, tropical grassland.

During the short rainy season, the savanna is green. At this time, grains and peanuts will grow. Most of the year, however, the savanna is dry and brown. Further north, the grass is drier still. Here nomad tribes keep their herds. Further north again, the grass ends, and the Sahara begins.

South of the savanna are tropical forests where heavy rains fall. Here some valuable crops are grown. They include kola nuts, cocoa, rubber, bananas, and palm oil.

It was in the Western Sudan that the African kingdoms of Ghana, Mali, and Songhai arose. They were located near the mountains where two great rivers have their sources.

▶ Find the Senegal (sen'ə gôl) and Niger (nī'jər) Rivers on the map on page 51. In which directions do they flow?

Why the Trading Kingdoms Grew in the Western Sudan

The African trading kingdoms began as settlements. The settlements were located along the banks of the Niger and Senegal

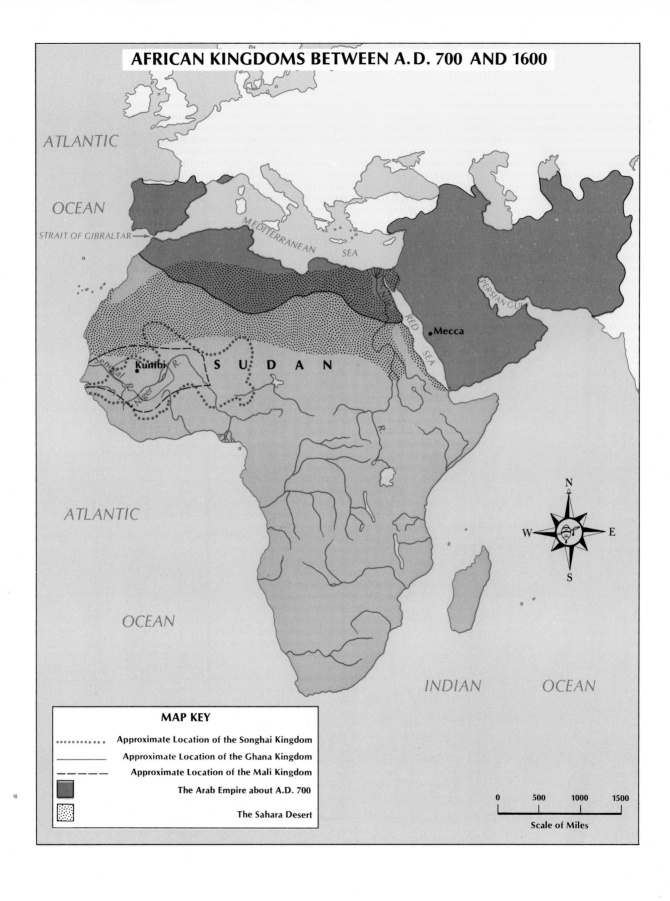

AFRICAN KINGDOMS BETWEEN A.D. 700 AND 1600

ATLANTIC

OCEAN

STRAIT OF GIBRALTAR

MEDITERRANEAN SEA

NILE

RED SEA

PERSIAN GULF

•Mecca

Senegal R.

Kumbi•

Niger R.

S U D A N

R.

ATLANTIC

OCEAN

INDIAN OCEAN

N
W E
S

MAP KEY

••••••••••   Approximate Location of the Songhai Kingdom

────────   Approximate Location of the Ghana Kingdom

── ── ──   Approximate Location of the Mali Kingdom

      The Arab Empire about A.D. 700

      The Sahara Desert

0   500   1000   1500

Scale of Miles

The Niger River in present-day Nigeria

Rivers. The people were able to use the rivers for trade. They traveled on the rivers to exchange goods with each other. There was another important advantage in a river location. The rivers were a reliable water supply for men and animals. With this water supply, a stable economy became possible. The river settlements could develop into cities. Slowly, a trading economy developed.

► Look at the map on page 51 showing the African kingdoms. Locate the Western Sudan. Locate the kingdoms of Ghana, Mali, and Songhai. Note how they overlap.

The dry grassland savanna of northern Nigeria

- Why do the boundaries of the three kingdoms overlap? (Clue: The map covers a period of 900 years.)

▶ What physical feature is a barrier between the kingdoms in the Western Sudan and the Islamic Empire in the north?

▶ Which rivers were important to the kingdoms of the Western Sudan?

▶ About how far is it from Ghana to the Nile? From Ghana to the Mediterranean Sea?

Iron ore was plentiful in the Western Sudan. It was in use by the third or fourth century A.D. The men of the Sudan were able to make iron farm tools and weapons. These tools and weapons were strong and lasting. Hoes and spades with iron heads were far better than those with wooden heads. With iron farm tools, men were able to produce a surplus of food. They were able to cultivate more land. Then the land could support more people. The population could grow. Civilization could develop.

With iron weapons, the men of the Sudan were better able to defend themselves. A warrior with an iron lance could usually beat a warrior with a wooden spear. A tribe that knew how to make iron weapons could give iron spears and swords to every warrior. Then powerful tribes could conquer weaker ones. More people and more territory could be brought under the rule of a single tribe. Then strong central government could begin.

Ghana and the Trade in Gold and Salt

Ghana probably started to develop in the second or third century A.D. At that time, nomads probably invaded the area and conquered the native tribes. About A.D. 700, the native tribes rebelled. They overthrew their nomadic rulers. The tribes were in power when the Arabs first appeared in the Sudan.

The Arab merchants set up trading settlements in Ghana. They established a trade in gold and salt that made Ghana wealthy. Gold came from Wangara (wän gä'rə), to the south of Ghana. The natives of Wangara needed salt in their diet. Salt had to be brought all the way from the Sahara. To get this salt, the natives of Wangara were willing to trade gold.

The kingdom of Ghana did not own either gold fields or salt mines. It simply controlled the caravan routes. All of these routes went through Ghana. That is why Ghana could make a profit. It became the **middleman** in the busy trade of salt for gold.

● How does the middleman in trade make a profit?

● To us, salt is one of the cheapest goods and gold is one of the most costly. Do you think the natives of Wangara had the same values? Why or why not?

● Find the modern nation of Ghana on a map. Is it located in the same place as ancient Ghana?

The exact location of Wangara was a secret. Today, scholars believe that it was in a forested area near the Senegal River. The natives of Wangara who mined the gold fields were a shy and primitive people. They traded for salt in a very curious way. We call it **silent barter**.

Salt is still mined in many places in Africa. Because salt is no longer rare, these salt slabs are no longer worth their weight in gold.

First the Arab merchants would come to Wangara. They were led there by guides from Ghana. The Arabs would leave supplies of salt, cloth, and other goods on the river banks. They would beat a drum to signal the natives of Wangara. Then they would go back a short way into Ghana. After the Arabs were gone, the natives of Wangara would cross the river. Next to each pile of goods, they would leave a pile of gold. Then they would go back across the river, and the Arabs would return. If the Arabs were satisfied with the amount of gold that had been left, they would beat the drum again. That showed that the trading was closed. If the Arabs were not satisfied, they would not beat the drum. They would not touch the piles of gold. Then the natives would have to leave more gold. All trading was done in this way. One side never met the other.

● Explain the meaning of *barter*. Is bartering usually done silently? How does the use of money make trading simpler?

In this trading, salt was just as important as gold. Salt was mined by slaves in a lonely Sahara desert town. It proved to be very profitable. Its value proved to be very steady. Slabs of salt were even used as money! Salt was the only good, or product, for which the natives of Wangara would always trade their gold.

● What is the difference between using salt as money and using it as a good? How did the Wangara people use it?

Government in Ghana

The ruler of Ghana was a king. The land of Ghana was divided into areas. Each area had a governor. The soldiers and workers were organized into classes. Each class had a special task.

To control its large territory, Ghana needed a strong ruler. It also needed a large army. The soldiers rode horses so that they could move quickly wherever they were needed. The army was supported by taxes. Taxes were paid by the Arab merchants and the smaller states under Ghana's control. The taxes also paid for the king's splendid court and for the costs of government.

Ghana set the pattern for later Sudanese kingdoms. These kingdoms had the same trading system. They too had large empires that kept expanding. They used a system of taxes similar to that of Ghana.

▶ What do we mean by *civilization?*

● Compare the rise of civilization in Ghana with the rise of civilization in other cultures, such as Sumer, or the Islamic Empire. (Use these ideas: *surplus product, division of labor, classes, cities, taxes, trade, invention, strong government, defense.*)

The kings of Ghana were all-powerful. In fact, the name *Ghana* means war chief. So the name of the country comes to us from the name given to its kings. The royal courts of Ghana were dazzling in splendor. One Arab writer described a Ghana court as follows:

When the king gives audience to his people, to listen to their complaints and set them to rights, he sits in a pavilion. Around the pavilion stand ten pages, holding shields and gold-trimmed swords. At his right hand are the sons of the princes of his empire, splendidly clad and with gold braided in their hair. The governor of the city is seated on the ground in front of the king. All around the governor are his counsellors. The gate of the chamber is guarded by dogs. They wear collars of gold and silver, ornamented with metal. The beginning of a royal audience is announced by the beating of a drum.

Centuries later, men were still writing about the splendor of the royal courts in Ghana. They told about royal feasts with as many as ten thousand guests. At these feasts, the king would give precious gifts to his subjects. They would ask the king to do special favors for them. He would listen, and say yes or no.

How the King Controlled the Gold

The wealth of Ghana was bound up with the power of the kings of Ghana. The kings had large armies and many servants. But they had something more. The people of Ghana believed that their king was a god. They believed that they would

The ruins of an Arab city in Africa

suffer if the king were sick. They would also suffer if his power grew weak. Their religious belief helped the king to keep his power strong.

★ Belief that rulers are gods or special agents of God has been common in the Human Adventure. What other examples can you think of?

Gold became plentiful in the kingdom of Ghana from the trading done by the merchants. It was so plentiful that it might have lost its value. The king stopped this from happening, however. He told his people that gold nuggets would harm them. He said that only a god—like himself—could handle the nuggets safely. The people handed all their nuggets over to the king. He owned every gold nugget in the empire. Some of these nuggets weighed over thirty pounds! Gold *dust*, however, was allowed to be used by the people. It served as the money of Ghana.

The king placed an export tax on gold. He collected this tax on every load of gold that left Ghana. This tax controlled the flow of gold out of the empire. On every load of salt that was brought into Ghana, the king placed an import tax. These taxes helped to keep the price of gold high.

● Why does the price of gold drop if too much gold is available?

★ What does *inflation* mean in economics? What happens to the value of money in times of inflation?

The Twin Cities of Kumbi

Ghana's capital was the city of Kumbi (kŭm' bē). Kumbi was really two cities. It was a royal city and a Muslim trading settlement. In the royal city was the king's palace—a fortress and several huts with rounded roofs, all enclosed by a wall. Near the palace was a forest. The people of Ghana believed a snake spirit lived in the forest. This spirit was important in their religion.

Six miles away from the royal city was the Muslim trading settlement. There were 30,000 Arabs living there. It was a large city for its time. The Arabs lived in low stone houses. They built twelve mosques. The people of Ghana allowed the Arabs to practice their religion freely.

Kumbi was the trading center of the empire. The market was crowded with cattle and sheep. Arabian horses were sold for use in Ghana's army. Sacks of grain and dried fruit were sold. So were pots of honey. Rolls of colorful cloth were on the counters. Leather goods, ivory, copper, and pearls were displayed in the stalls. Artists and craftsmen made jewelry, weapons, pottery, and clothing. Everything was paid for with gold dust.

Kumbi also supplied slaves to the Arabs and Europeans. Ghana made rich profits from slavery. In Africa, slavery was quite common. African slavery resulted mostly from tribal warfare. When strong tribes conquered weaker ones, they often used their captives as slave laborers. However, a slave in Africa did not have to stay a slave all his life. He could buy or work his way to freedom. Sometimes he could marry into the stronger tribe. Slaves had a place in the African community. They were seldom treated badly or sold away from their families.

★ How did Negro slavery in the New World differ from early African slavery?

Muslim Influence and the Downfall of Ghana

The Arabs brought to Ghana the culture and ideas of Islam. Under Arab influence, the people of Ghana enjoyed education and leisure. The royal court became more splendid than ever. The Arabs introduced three very important things to Ghana. These were a written language, the use of money and credit, and the Muslim code of law. Ghana did not adopt the Muslim religion, but later African kingdoms did. The people of Ghana were friendly with the Muslims. Friendship was first shown to the Muslim traders. Later, it was shown to Muslim scholars and other visitors. The ideas of Islam spread deeply into African culture.

The kingdom of Ghana lasted for almost a thousand years. Its downfall came in the eleventh century A.D. At that time, it was attacked by a nomadic tribe from the Sahara. They were a tribe of **Berbers**—poor but proud Muslims. The Berbers wanted a share in Ghana's wealth. Ghana held out against them for ten years of fierce fighting. Finally, however, Ghana was defeated. The kingdom was destroyed and many of the people were killed.

Soon the Berbers began fighting among themselves. Many small states tried to gain control of Ghana. In the late twelfth century, law and order came to an end in the Western Sudan. The caravan routes broke down. Trade became unsafe.

- Were the Berbers barbarians from Ghana's point of view? Explain.

- Do you think it likely that Ghana had been growing weak *before* the Berber invasion? Why or why not?

The winner in this struggle for power was the small state of Mali. Building on the ruins of Ghana, Mali created a kingdom that was even richer and more powerful. Mali's rise to power is the story of two great leaders—Sundiata (sun dē ä'tə) and Mansa Musa (män'sə mü'sə).

Sundiata—The Founder of Mali's Empire

Toward the end of the twelfth century, a cruel and ruthless leader had arisen in the Western Sudan. He was Sumanguru (sü' man gü' rü), king of the Sosso people. Sumanguru wanted to gain the power that Ghana had lost. He began by capturing the city of Kumbi. He made slaves of many of its people, and made them pay heavy taxes. Sumanguru's rule was so harsh that one tribe of Mali revolted against him. Led by Sundiata, this tribe defeated the armies of Sumanguru.

Sundiata became the first king of Mali. He is still honored as Mali's greatest national hero. After Sundiata defeated Sumanguru, he took over Ghana. New lands came under the rule of the kingdom of Mali. Under Sundiata, agriculture improved. The land once again began to yield a food surplus.

In many ways, the kingdom of Mali was like the kingdom of Ghana. Mali took Ghana's place as middleman in the trade in gold and salt. Mali, too, gained wealth and power this way. However, there was one important difference between the two empires. Soon after the Berber invasion, the people of Mali had given up their religion. They had become strong Muslims.

● For what reasons might the people of Mali have become Muslims?

● How might the controlling ideas of Islam affect the life of the people of Mali?

Under Sundiata, Mali rapidly became the most powerful empire in the Western Sudan. Still, it lacked a truly strong government and a system of law. It could not control the disorder and unrest in the Western Sudan. The golden age of Mali was not to come until the reign, or rule, of Mansa Musa. That was early in the fourteenth century.

The Reign of Mansa Musa

Under Mansa Musa, the kingdom of Mali covered a great land area. It was about as large as Western Europe. Mansa Musa opened a major new trade route to Cairo. He gained control of lands that were rich in copper. He brought important trading cities into the empire. He set up a system of government and restored law and order in the Western Sudan. He brought back the system of taxes that Ghana had developed. The smaller states under the control of Mali paid taxes to support the kingdom.

Mansa Musa was a great warrior. He was also a great statesman, and was interested in learning and the arts. Most important, he was a strong Muslim. During his reign, the culture of Islam mixed with the native African culture. The result was a new type of civilization marked by a strong feeling of law and justice.

From Mali, more and more Africans made pilgrimages to Mecca. In 1324, Mansa Musa himself set out on a pilgrimage. It was one of the most splendid journeys ever made. In front of the king marched 500 slaves. Each carried a bar of gold. The royal company numbered 60,000 men. In the caravan, a hundred camels carried sacks of gold dust. That was money to be spent along the way. Mansa Musa's pilgrimage gave most people their first look at Mali's wealth and power. Mali was recognized as a great power. Mansa Musa was recognized as a powerful ruler.

▶ Look at the map on page 51. Trace the route from Mali to Mecca. About how far is it?

▶ Why do Muslims make a pilgrimage to Mecca?

● Sometimes Mali is called a *kingdom,* sometimes an *empire.* What is the difference in meaning between the words?

The Decline of Mali and the Last Sudanese Kingdoms

Mansa Musa was a gifted and skillful leader. He was able to keep his subjects loyal. He was able to make the system of taxes work. The leaders who came after him were less skillful. After Mansa Musa's death in 1337, Mali slowly began to decline.

Mali had become almost too large to govern. In addition, trade and travel had taught other African peoples the skills of civilization. Iron tools and weapons were now used by many states and tribes inside and outside the empire.

Within Mali itself, increasing wealth and education led to restless feelings. The different peoples within the empire began to want independence. They did not want to pay taxes to a king in a distant capital. First the Songhai people rebelled. Other tribes followed. The Songhai were successful. After 1500, Mali was no longer an important kingdom.

● Twice in this chapter we have seen African examples of the ebb and flow of civilization. No one can say exactly what caused the civilization to ebb. How would *you* explain the decline of Mali and the decline of Ghana? (Consider: Were they both attacked by barbarians from outside? What things *inside* the empire-kingdoms might have

Medieval Europe was so impressed by the tremendous wealth of Mansa Musa that he was included on this fourteenth-century map. This section shows him holding a huge gold nugget while an Arab merchant rides in to trade with him. (Look again at the picture on page 48.)

weakened them? What, for example, do we mean when we say —"Mali had become almost too large to govern?" Why might wealth and education lead to restless feelings and demands for independence?)

The story of the medieval African kingdoms is still being uncovered. After the fall of Mali, power in the Western Sudan passed to the Songhai Empire. The Songhai Empire lasted until about 1600. In the end it was conquered by another power, and the kingdom of Songhai was destroyed.

★ Find out more on the history of Songhai and its rulers—Sunni Ali, and Askia the Great.

★ Find out about the Central Sudanese Kingdom of Kanem-Bornu (A.D. 800–1800).

EHQIPTI SIMVLACRA FVGVAT PRESENCIA XPI:

chapter 4

The Rise of Latin Christendom

We have seen how the Middle Ages got its name from historians in Western Europe. These historians thought that when the Roman Empire fell, civilization died out in Western Europe.

They were only partly right. During the early part of the Middle Ages, civilization *did* ebb in Western Europe. There were many barbarian invasions. There was continual fighting. Cities and towns were destroyed. Farms became battlefields. Learning and trade almost stopped. During these centuries, the light of civilization in Western Europe very nearly went out. That is why these early centuries of the Middle Ages are called the **Dark Ages**.

The Dark Ages lasted until about 1000. Then a new branch of civilization began to develop in Western Europe. In many ways, this branch of civilization is very close to us. It gave us many of our laws, our ideas, and our customs.

▶   What does the word *medieval* mean?

The influence of the Christian church is obvious in this ivory carving from thirteenth-century Germany.

Many different groups of people helped to form this new civilization. There were kings and great lords who lived in stone castles. There were brave knights, riding to battle in shining suits of armor. There were churchmen, who taught the people about Christianity. There were merchants and craftsmen who helped to restore trade, and to rebuild towns and cities. At the bottom of society, there were the peasants. They farmed the land.

The culture formed by the people of the Middle Ages was a mixture. In it, the ideas and traditions of Greece and Rome were blended with those of the Jews and Christians. Something else was added to this blend of ideas and traditions. That was the fighting spirit of the barbarians. The people of the Middle Ages loved to fight. They loved to have games of war. They loved to hear about heroes of the battlefield. Yet, at the same time, they loved beauty and peace. They wanted unity and order in their world.

Above all, these people were faithful Christians. They built hundreds of beautiful churches. They gave much of their surplus for church projects, and for works of charity. Sometimes they even went to war for their religion. In fact, they did not think of themselves as Europeans. To them, Europe was **Christendom** — the lands of Christ. They hoped that some day, all of Christendom would come under one church and one emperor. This dream never came true. Yet the idea and the name lasted for a long time.

▶ Look at the map of Christendom and Islam on page 67. Trace the area of Christendom. Was all of Europe part of Christendom? Was all of Spain in Christendom?

▶ Christendom was divided between two great churches. The Roman, or Latin, Catholic Church was centered in Rome. The Greek Orthodox Church was centered in Constantinople (now Istanbul). Find Rome and Constantinople on the map. Which part of Christendom was Latin? Which part was Greek?

The Middle Ages is an exciting period to study. As we turn back to these colorful days, let us keep a few questions in mind.

What happened to Western Europe after the fall of Rome? What did people do to survive during this time?

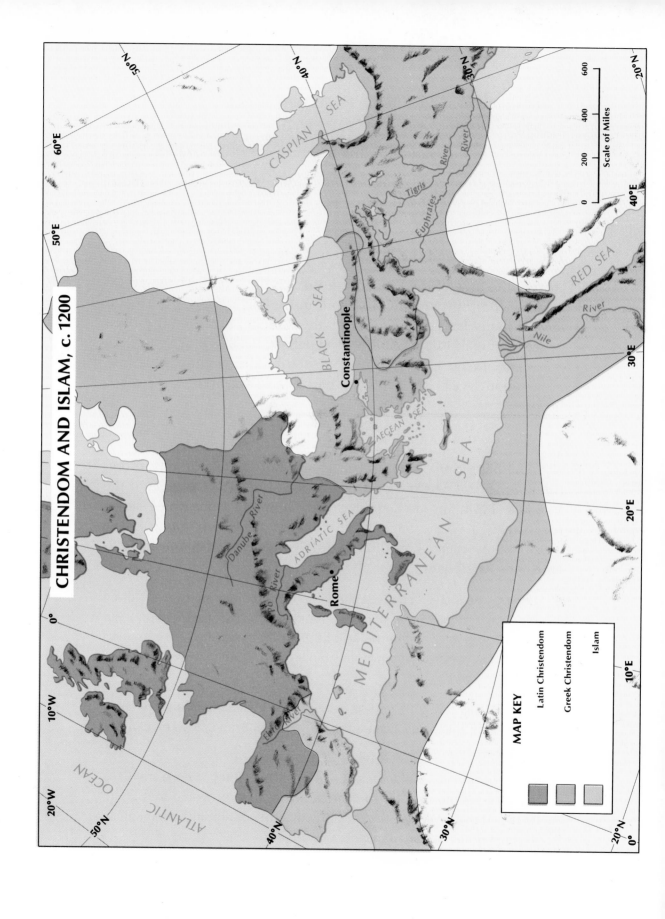

CHRISTENDOM AND ISLAM, c. 1200

MAP KEY

Latin Christendom

Greek Christendom

Islam

Scale of Miles

0   200   400   600

ATLANTIC OCEAN

MEDITERRANEAN SEA

ADRIATIC SEA

AEGEAN SEA

BLACK SEA

CASPIAN SEA

RED SEA

Rome

Constantinople

Danube River

Po River

Ebro River

Tigris River

Euphrates River

Nile River

What did men do to bring civilization back? What inventions helped them?

What was the culture of this new branch of civilization?

What did the civilization of the Middle Ages pass on to modern Western civilization?

The Dark Ages and the Problem of Defense

During the time of the Roman Empire, civilization had spread far into Western Europe. The Roman Empire had sent its armies and laws to many lands. Then, slowly, the Roman Empire in the West began to break down. Rome itself fell in A.D. 476. The Roman armies could no longer protect Western Europe from invasion. From about A.D. 500 to 1000, barbarians swept over Western Europe.

▶   What are the early centuries of the Middle Ages called?

The barbarians came into Western Europe from many directions. From the east and north came the Huns, the Goths, and the Vandals. From the area now called Germany came the Franks, the Angles, and the Saxons. The Franks gave their name to the country now called France. The Angles gave their name to England, or "Angle-land."

▶   Look at the map on page 69 showing the barbarian invasions. Notice how the barbarians swept over Western Europe, northeastern Europe, North Africa, and the Middle East. Imagine the suffering and confusion! What would happen to our civilization if it were invaded for centuries?

●   Name some earlier examples of barbarian invasions in history. How were such invasions connected with the ebb and flow of civilization?

●   What would the barbarians try to do after taking over a civilized country? Would they try to destroy civilization, or would they try to settle down? Would they find ways of defending themselves against other barbarian invaders? Explain.

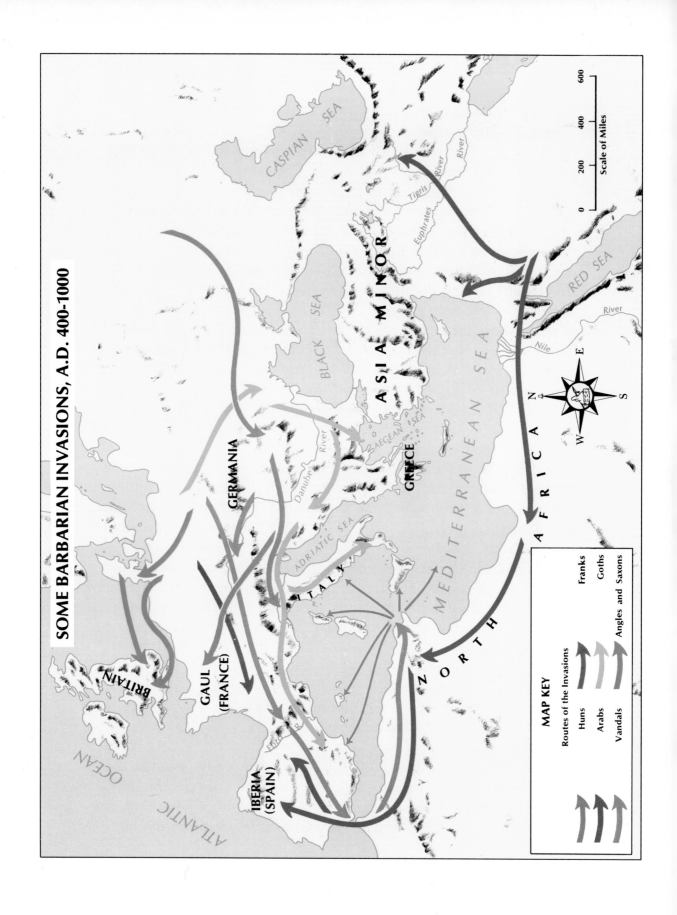

SOME BARBARIAN INVASIONS, A.D. 400-1000

ATLANTIC OCEAN

BRITAIN

GAUL
(FRANCE)

GERMANIA

IBERIA
(SPAIN)

ITALY

GREECE

ADRIATIC SEA

AEGEAN SEA

BLACK SEA

CASPIAN SEA

ASIA MINOR

MEDITERRANEAN SEA

NORTH AFRICAN

RED SEA

Nile River

Tigris River

Euphrates River

Danube River

Scale of Miles
0   200   400   600

N
W   E
S

MAP KEY

Routes of the Invasions

Huns

Arabs

Vandals

Franks

Goths

Angles and Saxons

Centuries of barbarian invasions does not seem like a good beginning for a great civilization. However, the barbarians really admired civilization. Once they had conquered an area, they wanted to set up a secure way of life. They wanted the conquered people to serve them and to grow their food.

Even then, however, the barbarians could not be sure of having a secure way of life. Different groups kept attacking each other's lands. Besides, there were always more barbarians on the outside. They just waited for a chance to come in. Bands of armed men kept raiding the fields and villages. The peasants could not grow their crops in safety.

In short, there was no safe law and order in Western Europe. No strong governments were left. There were only armed gangs. These gangs took anything they had the power to take. Only one organization was left to carry on the lessons of civilization. That was the Christian church in the West. This is usually called the Roman Catholic Church. We will call it the Latin Church because it was the church of Latin Christendom.

The Latin Church became powerful because many people joined it. Except for the Muslims in Spain, the barbarian settlers in all parts of Europe became Christians. The Latin Church kept the Christian faith alive in the West. It also kept alive some ideas from Greco-Roman culture.

The Latin Church was powerful, but it could not provide law and order. It could not defend the Europeans against barbarian attacks. The church had religious authority, but it had no armies or police. Besides, the heads of the church did not want to use force. If they tried to use force the church might lose its authority.

● What is *authority?* Explain why the church might lose its authority if it used armed force. Is this still true? Are certain ideas useless if people are forced to accept them?

In Western Europe, law and order were badly needed. So were some means of defense against barbarian attacks. In time, the problems of defense were solved. Along with a new kind of defender came a new kind of society. Let us see how this happened.

The Knight—A New Kind of Defender

During the Middle Ages, a new kind of fighter appeared. Barbarian warriors became **knights** on horseback. Eventually they became knights-in-armor.

Since ancient civilization, horses and mounted soldiers had been used in battle. Before the Middle Ages, however, the soldier on horseback was not a very effective fighter. He lacked two important inventions: *stirrups* (stėr'əps) and the *horseshoe*.

Barbarians from Central Asia first brought stirrups into Western Europe. Stirrups are attached to a horse's saddle to hold the rider's feet. Once a soldier had stirrups, he could sit firmly on a horse's back. Then he could charge against a strong line of foot soldiers. Without stirrups, a soldier on horseback could not make this sort of charge. As soon as he bumped into the line, he might fall off. Foot soldiers might knock him off with long spears.

After the stirrup came the horseshoe. Horseshoes are iron shoes made to be nailed to a horse's hoofs. They enable the horse to keep its footing in soft ground and to gallop over hard ground. With them, the horse can carry a heavy load and not damage its hoofs.

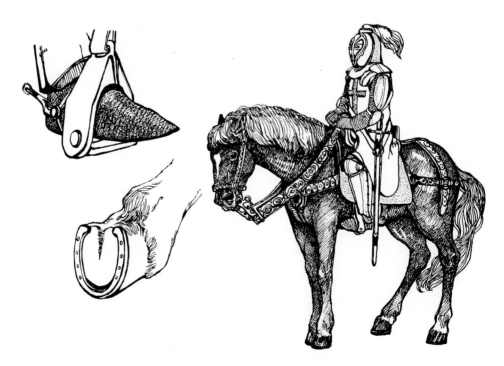

These three shields belonged to knights who took part in the early Crusades.

► Look at the pictures of knights-in-armor in this chapter. How much do you think their armor weighed? Without horseshoes, what would happen to a horse carrying a knight-in-armor over hard ground?

With these two important inventions, the fighting men of Western Europe could control the battlefield. This was especially true when they began to wear armor. The spears and arrows of the foot soldiers could seldom break through a knight's armor. Blows from foot soldiers could seldom make a knight fall from his horse. There were only two ways to make him fall. The saddle could be cut from his horse, or his horse could be killed. For protection, the knight's horse soon wore armor, too.

► Look again at the pictures of knights-in-armor. What parts of the horses are protected by armor? Explain why knights needed very strong and well-trained horses.

● It was costly to be a heavily armored soldier in classical Greece. Would it be more or less costly to be a medieval knight-in-armor? Explain.

● During the Dark Ages, could taxes have been collected to pay for an army of knights? (Remember: Most cities and towns and farms had been destroyed. There was no central government.)

Each knight-in-armor wore a coat made of heavy links of iron. On top of this coat he wore iron or steel plates. These plates protected his shoulders, chest, arms, and legs. His head was covered by an iron or steel helmet. The helmet had a movable facepiece. Even the knight's hands were protected. He wore strong, iron gloves. When a knight put on all of his armor, it was hard to tell who he was. For identification, he carried a battle shield. His "coat-of-arms" was painted on this shield. The coat-of-arms told what family he came from.

The armor worn by the knight in the fifteenth-century tapestry above was probably not really in use at that time. The artist just used his imagination to make his tapestry more interesting.

A lot of time and money was spent making the suit of armor at left. It belonged to an English nobleman and was constructed completely of steel.

Ball-and-chain

Three types of daggers

A knight-in-armor knew how to use several weapons. To smash the armor of an enemy knight, he could use a battle-axe or a ball-and-chain. To kill his enemy, he could use a sharp dagger and a two-handed sword. His most important weapon was a long, heavy spear called a lance. In battle, many knights would line up together on their horses. Then, pointing their lances forward, they would rush toward their enemies. The line of knights would rush forward like a thundering wall of iron. From fighters like these, Western Europe gained the defense it needed so badly.

With the knights providing defense, the peasants could grow and harvest crops. There were economic and political problems, however. Supporting a large force of knights required the work of many people. That is how the need for defense gave rise to a new society and a new economy. A whole new way of life developed. We call this way of life the **feudal** (fū′dl) **system**.

The Feudal System—A New Way of Life

The feudal system was based on the ownership of land. As the feudal system developed, most of the land in Western Europe came under the control of **lords**. During the early years of the feudal system, nearly all the lords had once been knights. They became lords simply by becoming more powerful than other knights. They used their power to claim land and the title of lord. Then, as time went on, most lords were lords by birth. They gained their lands and titles through their families.

When a lord had become powerful enough, he set up his own government. All over Western Europe, there were hundreds of such governments. Each lord had his own army of knights. The lord and his knights defended the land against raiders.

The highest duty of a knight was to his lord. He swore that he would be loyal to his lord. He swore that he would help him whenever he was needed. In return, the knight usually received a piece of land from his lord. This land was called a **fief** (fēf).

The lords and their ladies lived in stone castles. Most often, a lord built his castle for defense. He had to be able to protect himself against attacks from his enemies. That is why he would build his castle with towers and thick stone walls. Many of his knights lived at the castle and helped to defend it.

The peasants lived in villages close to the castle. Their homes were small, crude huts. The peasants farmed the land, and were very poor. Sometimes enemy knights would come to rob their villages. When that happened, the peasants would hurry to their lord's castle. There, behind the stone walls, they were better protected. They had to pay for protection from the lord and his knights, however. The peasants had to obey their knight or lord. Since they had very little money, they paid in goods and services.

The peasants were not the only ones to give goods and services for protection. The same thing happened at other levels of the feudal system. Any landholder under the protection of someone else was called a **vassal** (vas'l). Therefore, a knight was a vassal to his lord. A lesser lord was a vassal to a greater lord.

Look at the diagram of the feudal system on the next page. The actual feudal system was much more complex than this simple

THE FEUDAL SYSTEM

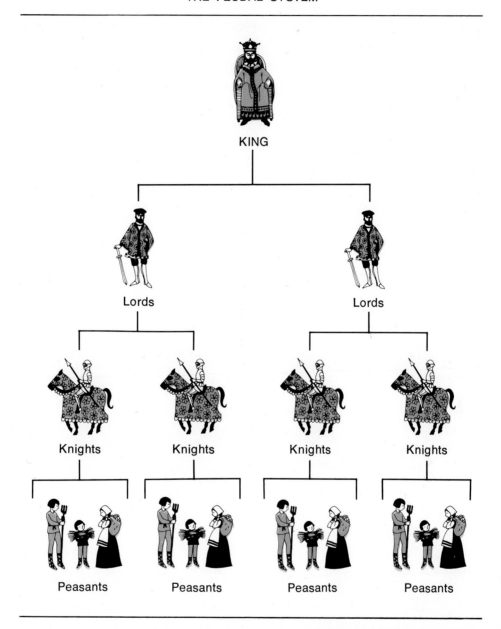

diagram. Often there was a king with great lords beneath him. There were lesser lords beneath the great lords, and then even lesser lords beneath them. Next in importance to the lords were the knights and their servants. At the bottom of society were the farmers, or peasants.

As time went on, several lords would join together under some great lord or king. This gave them even greater protection. Still, kings did not become powerful for a long time. Until they did, the lords were the most powerful leaders in the feudal system. A great lord could be under the king's rule. Yet, he might own more land than the king. He might have a larger army of knights. The great lords did not want a strong king. They knew that a strong king would take away much of their power.

A feudal king had only a small army of his own. When he needed a larger army, he asked the great lords to bring their knights to help him. The lords had to pledge allegiance to the king, but the knights did not. Each knight pledged loyalty only to his lord. If his lord were killed in battle, a knight did not have to keep on fighting for the king.

In the medieval drawing on the opposite page peasants are busy harvesting in the fields outside their lord's castle walls. The Italian castle above is not as elaborate, but it was built as a strong fortress and has survived since 1340.

- Why do you think the lords did not want to have a strong king? What are some ways in which a king might become a stronger ruler than any of the lords?

Obviously, the feudal system was very different from a society such as the one we live in. You will notice some important differences as you answer the following questions.

- As citizens of the United States, to what or to whom do you pledge allegiance? If you were a knight in the feudal system, to whom would you pledge allegiance?

- As citizens of the United States, to what or to whom do your parents pay taxes? If your parents were peasants in the feudal system, to whom would they owe goods and services?

- As citizens of the United States, to what or to whom might you have to give military service? As a knight in the feudal system, to whom would you have to give military service?

The New Agriculture

Before the people of Latin Christendom could get on with the work of building a civilization, they had to grow a large surplus of food.

▶   Why is a surplus needed for civilized living?

To grow a large surplus, they had to overcome a new problem. The problem was especially difficult in the northwestern part of Europe. The climate of northwestern Europe is very humid. A great deal of rain and mist is brought by the west winds from the Atlantic. The soil is good for growing crops. However, it is wet and heavy.

At first, the farmers in northwestern Europe used a light plow. It was like the plow used by the Greeks and Romans. This kind of plow was fine for turning the dry, light soil of the Mediterranean region. In northwestern Europe, however, this plow was not strong enough. It could not break up the wet, heavy soil of the valleys and plains. People were forced to farm the poorer soil on the hills.

Then a new plow came into use. This plow was heavy. It had wheels. It had an iron knife to cut the soil. Behind the knife was a plowshare. The **plowshare** was a blade that dug into the soil. Attached to the plowshare was a moldboard. The **moldboard** turned the soil over. This plow was much like the plow used today by farmers in northwestern Europe and North America.

With this new plow, farmers in Western Europe could cultivate the rich soils of the valleys and plains. The new plow had another advantage, too. As the moldboard turned the soil, it left a ridge and a furrow. Each ridge was like a long, tiny hill running

A medieval French artist showed only two oxen pulling the plow, but in other ways his drawing is accurate. Such an illustration proves that the new plow was known in France at that time.

through the field. Each furrow was like a long, tiny valley. Extra water would ooze down into the furrows. Then it could flow off the field. This kept young plants from being drowned by extra water.

From four to eight oxen were needed to pull the heavy plow. It was best used for plowing long, narrow strips. First the oxen would pull the plow one way along a strip of land. Then they would rest while the plow was turned around. Then the oxen would pull the plow back. They would make another furrow right beside the first one.

The invention of the heavy plow is another example of how men make progress. Once again, men experimented. Once again, they found a new way to develop a new civilization.

The Manor

In many parts of Western Europe, the feudal system plus the new way of farming led to something else new. They led to a different kind of farming community. This new community was called a **manor** (man'ər).

We have read how land was divided under the feudal system. Each lord divided his land among his lesser lords and knights. The lesser lords and knights divided their land into smaller areas, or manors. Each manor was farmed by the peasants of one village. The peasants lived in little huts near the fields. They worked the fields for themselves and for the lord of the manor. In the village, there was the lord's manor house or small castle. There was also a tiny church with a priest.

Around the village were the long, straight fields. All the peasant families helped to farm the fields that belonged to the lord of the manor. They also helped to farm some for the village priest. The rest of the land was divided among the families for their own use.

There were few towns where people of the manors could go to buy goods or services. Besides, few people had money to buy anything. Instead, they ground their own grain into flour. They made their own shoes and clothing. They repaired their own tools. The peasants grew just enough food to support themselves and their protectors.

- The manor fitted in perfectly with the feudal system and the rough life of the Middle Ages. Would it fit in with a more advanced way of life? Explain.

- By 1100, the peasants of the manor were producing more of a surplus in crops and goods. What was likely to happen when the surplus grew large enough to support many skilled workers, such as builders, artists, or merchants? Consider the following possibilities:

division of labor	money
capital (savings)	schools
trade	sculpture
towns	taxes
great buildings	stronger government by kings

chapter 5

The Culture of Latin Christendom

People in one branch of civilization are different from the people in another branch. They are different because they each have a *different culture*. They each have a *different pattern of social behavior*.

A people's culture is largely the result of their controlling ideas. These controlling ideas may be about God. They may be about the nature of the world and the universe. They may be about the purpose of life. To understand the people, we must learn about their culture. We must learn what their controlling ideas are.

- Explain what is meant by *controlling ideas*. Why are such ideas important? Name some of the controlling ideas you have studied.

The feudal system gave men of the Middle Ages a good way to defend themselves. This made it possible for people to spend time on agriculture. Then they could grow a surplus of food. The surplus enabled men to trade. The growth of trade led them into contact with other people and other cultures. Latin Christendom began to develop a civilization of its own.

Goblins, Witches, and Deep, Dark Forests

In the Middle Ages, the population of Western Europe was small. Much of the land was untouched by man. Roads were very poor. Travel was slow and dangerous. Most of the manors were little worlds in themselves. They were surrounded by deep, dark forests and swamps. Sometimes only a tiny path led through the forest from one manor or village to another.

The lord of the manor would often go into the forest to hunt wild boars and deer. Most peasants were afraid of the forest, however. They knew that robbers often hid there. They thought that terrible giants, goblins, and witches lived there. At night, wolves howled in the distance. The peasants would shiver around tiny fires in their cottages. Someone would tell a story about the magic creatures of the forest. The story might be about a prince who was turned into a frog. It might be about children who were lost in the forest and captured by a witch. If you have ever read any of Grimm's fairy tales, you know the kinds of stories the peasants would tell. Such stories made the peasants more afraid of the forest than ever!

★ In England, the peasants loved to hear stories about Robin Hood, a robber who lived in the woods. According to the stories, Robin Hood robbed the rich to give to the poor. Read some stories about Robin Hood and his Merry Men. Do you think there really *was* a Robin Hood?

The Age of Chivalry

Life in the great castles was quite different from life in the manor house and village. During the Middle Ages, the great lords and ladies and their knights set up a new style of behavior. It was called chivalry (shiv'əl rē). **Chivalry** means the way of life of knights.

This fourteenth-century knight is shown in ceremonial splendor. He is being handed his helmet and shield by the ladies he has sworn to protect.

To become a knight, a boy had to be from a **noble** family—a family of lords and ladies. Usually a boy would begin his training for knighthood when he was about seven. First he became a *page* and helped the ladies of a lord's castle. As a page, he would serve at the feasts held for the knights. Next he became a *squire* and learned to fight and hunt. When he was about 20, he could become a knight. As a knight, he was ready to fight whenever there was need for him to fight. A knight had to be tough. He had to know all the skills of battle. One way of practicing these skills was by mock battles called **tournaments** (tėr′nə mənts).

THE CODE OF CHIVALRY

A Knight was:

1. Loyal to his Lord.

2. Faithful to the Lady he loved.

3. Loyal to the Church.

4. A protector of the weak, the poor, the helpless, and all women and children.

5. A brave and well-trained fighter, and could bear great suffering and hardship.

6. Fair, just, kind, truthful.

As time went on, this rough soldier's code developed into something quite different. It was the beginning of our own Western ideas of good manners. How did this happen? As Latin Christendom grew more civilized, the meaning of chivalry changed. A good knight had to be more than a brave fighter. He had to be polite as well. He had to show the highest loyalty to the persons he served. He could never break a promise. He could never shrink from his duty—even if it meant giving up his life!

A good knight was loyal to the church. He was kind and gentle to the weak and the wounded. It was his duty to protect any lady from danger. Of course, few knights lived up to all these ideals. Still, the pattern was set. To this day, a "gentleman" is judged, in part, by standards of chivalry.

Christianity was also a great influence in changing manners. Jesus had taught that people should be loving. In the eyes of God, he said, women are equal to men. The Catholic Church taught people to love and honor Mary, the mother of Jesus. Lessons such as these helped to form a new code of behavior. It was different from the codes of all earlier cultures.

Of course, the change in behavior did not take place quickly. It did not affect everyone. All knights did not keep their promises. All women were not treated kindly. Still, a new set of ideas did come into being. The ideas are still with us.

The Stories of Chivalry

In the Middle Ages, the lords and ladies held great feasts in their huge castle halls. Often, these feasts were to honor their knights. During the feasts, they would listen to stories about famous battles and brave heroes. Many of these heroes were real people in history. Yet most of the stories about the heroes were made up by the story-tellers. Even so, these stories tell us much about medieval people and their culture. They tell us what people liked to hear. They describe the deeds that people most admired.

● Think about some of the myths, stories, and legends you have read. What kinds of things have they told you about the people and their cultures?

● Make a list of the kinds of stories that you most like to read or see in the movies or on television. Do you like stories about spies, cowboys, or spacemen? How would you describe the heroes of such stories? Are they clever and brave? What other qualities do they have?

Let us read a story about Roland, a famous hero of the age of chivalry. From the story, we can learn much about such heroes. We can learn what the important things in life were to medieval people.

THE SONG OF ROLAND

Long ago in France, twelve daring and handsome knights faithfully served the mighty Emperor Charlemagne (shär'lə mān). The knights were famous for their brave deeds and for their skill in battle. Dressed in shining armor, they rode beside the emperor wherever he went. To the people of France, they were known as the Twelve Peers of Charlemagne. (In former times, a peer was a companion.)

The most famous of the Twelve Peers was a young count named Roland. Roland was a perfect knight in all that he did. He feared no enemy. Roland was also kind and generous. He loved his vassals as if they were his own brothers.

Roland had an evil stepfather named Ganelon (gan'ə lon). Ganelon was very jealous of Roland's fame and wealth. One day Ganelon led Roland into a terrible trap.

Some time earlier, Charlemagne's forces had crossed the Pyrenees (pir'ə nēz) Mountains into Spain. There they had defeated the troops of a Muslim king. After the battle, Charlemagne sent Ganelon to the Muslim camp. He told him to collect great treasures from the defeated enemy. This would show that the Muslims accepted their defeat. Ganelon had other plans, however. As soon as he met the Muslim king, he told him how he might win back his land.

"Tomorrow Charlemagne will return to France," Ganelon said to the king. "He will leave a small army to guard the pass behind him. I will make sure that this army is made up of the Twelve Peers and their vassals. Your forces can easily attack them at the pass. When you have killed the Twelve Peers, Charlemagne will be senseless with grief. He will not have the heart to go into battle. Then you can take back your lands in peace."

The Muslim king was delighted with the plan. He rewarded Ganelon with beautiful armor, jewels, and other riches. Ganelon returned to Charlemagne's camp and arranged to have the Twelve Peers lead the rear guard.

So it was that the next day, the Twelve Peers went to guard the pass. There they came face to face with hundreds of thousands of Muslim soldiers. Oliver, one of Roland's best friends, cried out in disbelief. "Surely the traitor Ganelon has sold our bones to the Muslims! There are countless numbers of them waiting to attack! Pray,

In one of the cathedrals of France there is a stained-glass window which honors the memory of Roland. This section of that window shows Roland twice, as he tries to break his sword and finally blowing his famous horn for help. The Muslims he has killed lie beneath his feet.

Roland, blow your horn loudly across the mountain peaks. Charlemagne will hear. He will return with his troops to help us."

Roland refused to blow his horn. He said, "I will not bring dishonor on the names of the Twelve Peers by calling for help." The Christian knights fought bravely. Roland had a sword that he called Durandel (dū ran del'). Using it, he cut off the head of every Muslim who dared fight him. Many Christians were killed. The Muslims also suffered great losses, but still they outnumbered the Christians.

When the Archbishop saw that all the French soldiers would soon be dead, he rode up beside their leader. "Roland," he said, "it is too late for Charlemagne to save the lives of these daring soldiers. But if you blow your horn, the emperor will get here in time to give them a Christian burial. We must not let their bodies be torn apart by the dogs and the wolves." Roland put his horn to his lips and blew it so loud that the mountains seemed to tremble.

"Hark! That is Roland's horn!" cried Emperor Charlemagne. "Our men are in battle."

Ganelon quickly answered, "How could that be? I assure you the Muslims want peace. This must be some trick of Roland's."

Just then they heard the horn again. Then, Charlemagne knew there was trouble. He knew that Ganelon was a traitor. He had him arrested and promised him a most horrible death for betraying the emperor and Christendom.

Charlemagne blew his own horn to answer Roland. His horn call was so loud that the Muslims heard it and fled. But, alas, Roland was the only Frenchman left alive. Badly wounded and filled with grief, Roland carried the bodies of his valiant men away from the field of battle. He laid them gently on the grass. Seeing Muslim blood on the blade of his sword, Durandel, Roland was filled with fury. He began to pound the sword against a large stone. "Let no wicked Muslim steal this sword," he cried in despair. "No Muslim will use my sword Durandel against a Christian!" But the sword was made so well that Roland could not destroy it. Instead, he laid it on the ground and covered it with his body. And there on the hillside Roland died.

When Charlemagne and his troops arrived, they were amazed to see how many Muslims had been killed. Tears came to their eyes when they saw that all the Frenchmen were dead. Charlemagne pulled the whiskers of his flowing white beard in despair. Then suddenly he shouted his famous battle cry, "Mountjoy! Mountjoy! After those people! May God help us revenge the death of the Twelve Peers and their vassals!"

With that, the French troops set out after the Muslims, killing them, destroying their mosques and their cities, and sweeping them off the land.

- Why do you think Roland gave his sword a name?

- Why did Roland refuse to blow his horn at first? In the same situation, what would you have done? Why?

- What made Roland change his mind about blowing his horn? What does this tell you about his faith?

- Do you think Roland died bravely? Do you think the people of the age of chivalry liked such an ending? Explain.

- What did the Christians think of the Muslims? What do you suppose the Muslims thought of the Christians?

- What other things about chivalry have you learned from this story?

The Rise of Towns

By 1100, great changes had taken place in northwestern Europe. This was centuries after the time of Roland and Charlemagne. The forests were no longer quite so dark and deep as they had been. Much more of the land had been cleared for farming. The population was growing. The new agriculture was giving a surplus. Breeds of horses and cattle had been improved. Sheep farming had become important to the economy. Before long, the herds of sheep were providing peasants with two important things. They were providing a supply of meat, and they gave wool for clothing.

With the growth in the economy, men were able to specialize in different kinds of work. The first men to specialize were blacksmiths, carpenters, and other skilled workers. At first, they went from manor to manor to do their work. Later, they found it was better to settle in one place. As these craftsmen settled down, towns began to rise. The few towns that survived from Roman days began to grow again.

● To defend themselves against raiders, the townsmen built high walls around their towns. Why don't we have high walls built around modern cities?

This medieval walled town still exists in the harbor of Concarneau, France.

Fritzlar had already become a prosperous German town when this drawing was completed. Notice that it is surrounded by high walls.

As the towns grew and prospered, so did trade. Trade was made possible by the larger surplus of food and wool. The wool was sold to clothmakers in the towns. The clothmakers in turn would spin the wool and weave it into cloth. Some of the cloth was sold. Some was made into clothing and then sold.

Other goods began to appear in the markets. Furs were shipped from Norway and Sweden. A great wine trade began in France. Metals were mined. The supply of iron in Latin Christendom was far greater than it had been even in classical Greece and Rome. Tin, lead, silver, and gold were also plentiful. By the twelfth century, Western Europe was again trading with the Middle East. The trading ships of Italian city-states sailed back and forth across the Mediterranean.

What a change all this was from the dangerous, confusing times of the Dark Ages! As towns grew and trade increased, governments became stronger. The church became powerful and well organized. New learning and art came into Latin Christendom from Islam. Schools and universities were established. Beautiful, large cathedrals were built. By 1100, the light of civilization had grown bright again. The Dark Ages had passed.

A great many magnificent churches were constructed during the thirteenth century. The medieval drawing at left gives us some idea of building methods. Because a woman gave large amounts of money to the church to help with such projects, her likeness was included in a stained-glass window.

Education and Art in Latin Christendom

The people of Latin Christendom were very strong in their faith. This led them to give much of their wealth for the glory of God. They gave money to the church and to the poor. They gave money to set up schools and universities. From these beginnings, learning began to spread. The spread was very gradual. Churchmen and, much later, merchants and government officials learned how to read and write. More and more stories, poems, and plays were written. Most of these writings were religious.

From the art of the later Middle Ages, we can learn much about Latin Christendom. We can learn about its controlling ideas. Most of the art was closely tied to Christianity. In fact, the finest works of the medieval artists and craftsmen went into the great cathedrals and churches.

During the Middle Ages, French craftsmen invented a new style of architecture. It was called **Gothic architecture**. Gothic architecture was very different from any architecture that had come before. In earlier times, the roofs of the churches had been held up by thick, strong walls. The church builders had put few windows in the walls. They knew that the walls would be stronger without windows. Then French builders learned to hold up the roof of a cathedral in a new way. They found that they could use pointed arches. To support these arches, they used strong, stone props. These props were called **buttresses**.

★ Find out what *buttress* and *flying buttress* mean. See if you can find pictures of pointed arches, buttresses, and flying buttresses of the Gothic cathedrals.

Flying buttresses such as these were absolutely necessary to provide support for the tall, narrow arches that medieval architects invented and loved to build. Left, the interior of Bourges cathedral in France.

MEDIEVAL ART

Medieval artists were excellent storytellers. Usually they were inspired by stories from the Bible, but they often included details from their own observations of nature.

Left, in the twelfth century this statue of Mary and Jesus was carved out of wood and then painted.

Below, a stone carving of Eve picking the forbidden fruit in the Garden of Eden.

Right, the same sculptor used giant hands to carry this unhappy sinner to Hell.

Far right, a tapestry

Bottom right, a carving on a stone pillar shows the Devil and St. Peter watching the fall of Simon.

Some of the most beautiful stained-glass windows in the world were constructed in France in the twelfth and thirteenth centuries. This window tells stories from the life of the medieval king, Charlemagne.

With pointed arches and buttresses, the French builders could build tall cathedrals. The cathedrals seemed to reach straight up to heaven. The walls could have huge windows. Craftsmen made these windows out of bits of brightly colored glass. We call it **stained glass**. As the light came through the windows from the outside, they seemed to be made of beautiful, bright jewels. Most of the windows showed pictures that told Bible stories. In those days, ordinary people could not read. The pictures in these stained-glass windows helped them remember the teachings of their Christian faith.

● Look at the pictures of the different kinds of medieval art shown in this chapter. How does this art differ from Greek art? From Muslim art? From the art of today?

These stone figures have watched over the central door of Chartres cathedral in France for more than 800 years.

● Do the figures in the sculpture and painting look like real human beings? Can you explain why the medieval artists did not try to show real things? Why didn't they try to make sculpture like that of the Greeks?

chapter 6

Religion and Government in Latin Christendom

In Latin Christendom, the strongest controlling ideas came from the Christian faith. These ideas affected all parts of the people's lives—including their form of government. In medieval times there was only one church in Latin Christendom. That was the Roman Catholic Church. The church was deeply respected. The highest person in the church was the **pope.** Then came the other high churchmen—the archbishops and bishops.

These high churchmen were helped by men and women who joined religious orders, or groups. Some of these men and women were friars (fri′ ərz) and sisters of mercy. Some were teachers. Some cared for the sick and the poor. Some were monks and nuns who spent their lives in **monasteries** and **convents.** There they worked, and prayed, and copied ancient books. There were even religious orders of knights. They went to battle for the church.

Life in the Middle Ages was not easy.

The Age of Faith

Many people of the Middle Ages felt that the church was like an army. They felt that it must fight to save the souls of men and women. They felt this way because of their belief in God and the devil.

People feared and hated the devil. They felt that the church must fight a never-ending war against him. Church services became daily battles against sin. Church buildings protected the towns and villages where Christians lived. They protected the fields where Christians worked. They protected the churchyards where Christians were buried.

The Middle Ages has been called the "Age of Faith." This is a good description. It reminds us that people felt they were caught in a battle between good and evil. To help them win the battle, they wanted a strong church. That is why they did not like anyone who disagreed with the church. To them, such people were doing the work of the devil.

Sometimes the church asked kings and nobles to punish people who had wrong ideas about religion. In the Age of Faith, such punishment seemed only natural. The people felt that they could not risk disagreements about religion. People who did not agree with the teachings of the church were harshly punished. In particular, the Jews suffered greatly. In 1348, a terrible disease swept through Europe. It was called the Black Death. Thousands of people died. In many towns, the Christians blamed the Jews for the disease. They falsely accused them of poisoning the drinking water. They drove some Jews out of their towns. They burned others at the stake. Some of these Jews were wealthy merchants and moneylenders. The Christians took over all their belongings.

- Do you think such actions were according to the teachings of Christ? Why do you think the Jews were treated as they were? Explain.

The Crusades

Many knights of Latin Christendom fought for their religious faith. Some fought against the Muslims in Spain. Others fought in a series of holy wars. There were eight of these wars in all, lasting from 1096 to 1274. They were called **crusades**, a name that meant Wars for the Cross.

The crusaders meet a band of Muslims.

The crusades began when the Byzantine Empire needed help. The Byzantine Empire was the eastern branch of Christendom. It was being invaded by Turks who were Muslims. The empire needed help to fight the Turks who were already in control of Palestine and Syria. They made it very difficult for any Christian pilgrims to visit Jerusalem. Jerusalem was a holy city of Christianity. It was in Palestine which was often called the Holy Land. In 1095, the pope called for a holy war to capture Jerusalem from the Muslims.

► Why would Christian pilgrims want to visit Jerusalem?

The Third Crusade began in 1187 because Saladin, the most famous Muslim warrior of the twelfth century, had captured Jerusalem. To free the Holy Land, crusaders, including the kings of both England and France, fought against him. This manuscript shows one of their bloody battles.

Religious faith led many Western Europeans to join the crusades. Many died of sickness and hunger on the way to Eastern Europe and Palestine. However, the First Crusade was successful. It was led by French noblemen. For a time, the French lords set up feudal governments in Palestine and Syria. Then, in 1187, the Muslims reconquered Jerusalem. Once again they took over Palestine and Syria. Later crusades failed to drive them out.

The crusades show us the power of religious faith in Latin Christendom. Yet some of the crusaders did not really seem to be fighting for the Cross. They seemed more interested in other things—especially in looting and adventuring. The Fourth Cru-

Fortresses were constructed along the routes to Jerusalem to shelter and protect the crusaders. This castle, built between the eleventh and the thirteenth century, still stands on the coast of Turkey.

sade, for instance, resulted in the capture of Constantinople. The soldiers of the cross sacked this Christian city and killed thousands of its people. Another instance was the Children's Crusade. Many young people set out to march to Jerusalem. They never got past southern France, however. There they were captured by their fellow Christians and sold into slavery!

The crusades show us that the culture of Latin Christendom was complicated. Christians were fighting to drive the Muslims out of the Holy Land. Yet, at the same time, Christian scholars were eagerly studying Muslim ideas. Christian knights were trained to give their lives for ladies in distress. Yet they were also trained in the fighting spirit of the barbarian invaders. Western Europe was still not strongly governed. Feudal adventurers were still ready to set off on warlike expeditions.

To the emperor in Constantinople, the crusades often seemed like one more barbarian invasion. He had to face two sets of invaders. There were the Muslims, invaders from the East. There were the crusaders, invaders from the West. The emperor could not be sure which set of invaders was the more frightening.

The Little Brothers of the Poor

In the Age of Faith, not all battles against the devil were fought with swords. Some were fought by prayer and by the example of a holy life. One hero of the Age of Faith was a friar named Francis of Assisi (äs sē'zē).

Francis was born about the year 1182. His father was a rich merchant in the city of Assisi, in northern Italy. As a young man, Francis lived a carefree life. Then, while serving as a soldier, he was captured and put in prison. There he became very ill. He began to think about the purpose of life. He decided to give up the life of a rich young man.

Francis wanted to live just as Jesus had lived. He gave away his handsome clothes and his money and became a beggar. The only thing he owned was the ragged robe he wore. He spent the rest of his life helping the poor and the sick. Francis believed that God had called him to this service.

Soon other men began to admire the work that Francis was doing. They gave up everything they had and joined him. The pope gave Francis and his followers permission to become a religious order. They called themselves the Franciscans (fran sis' kənz). Many people called them the "little brothers of the poor."

Francis taught his followers to love all people, all animals, all plants. To him, everything in God's creation was worthy of love. All things were brothers and sisters. Once he wrote a poem thanking God for "brother sun" and "sister moon," for "brother wind" and "sister water," for "brother fire" and "sister mother earth." One legend tells how Francis preached, or spoke, to the sparrows.

FRANCIS AND THE SPARROWS

One day Francis was walking near a field with another Franciscan. He saw several birds singing in a nearby tree, and he said, "Brother, wait for me here. I must go and preach to the sparrows."

Francis went to the tree, and the little birds flew down and gathered around his feet. Some even perched on his head and shoulders to show their trust in him.

A painting of St. Francis of Assisi by Bellini (detail)

Francis said, "Sister sparrows, you must always praise the Lord. He has given you wings to fly with, streams from which you may drink, trees in which you may build your nests, and food for you to eat. God created you. He loves you and has given you many things. You must always thank Him."

The sparrows spread their wings and showed him that they understood. With great joy, Francis blessed them and made the sign of the cross over them. Suddenly, the birds flew into the air and formed a cross in the sky. Then some of the birds flew to the east, while others flew to the west, to the north, and to the south. Francis took this to be God's sign that he and his brothers should teach the word of God in all parts of the world.

- Do you think that Francis lived up to the teachings of Jesus? Explain.

- Have you read of other holy men who can be compared with Francis? Tell about them.

- How does the life of Francis reveal one of the controlling ideas of Latin Christendom?

Government in Latin Christendom

We have read many times that there is a tension in Western culture. It is a tension between Judeo-Christian and Greco-Roman

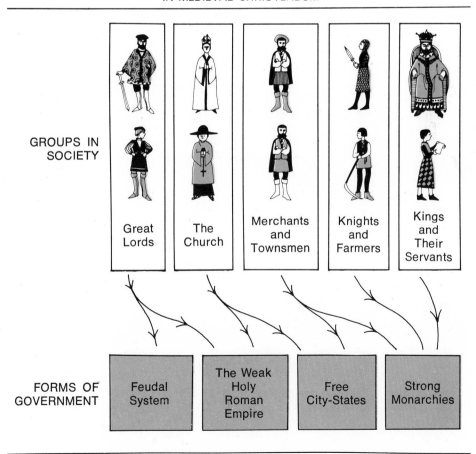

FORMS OF GOVERNMENT WANTED BY DIFFERENT GROUPS
IN MEDIEVAL CHRISTENDOM

GROUPS IN SOCIETY

| Great Lords | The Church | Merchants and Townsmen | Knights and Farmers | Kings and Their Servants |

FORMS OF GOVERNMENT

| Feudal System | The Weak Holy Roman Empire | Free City-States | Strong Monarchies |

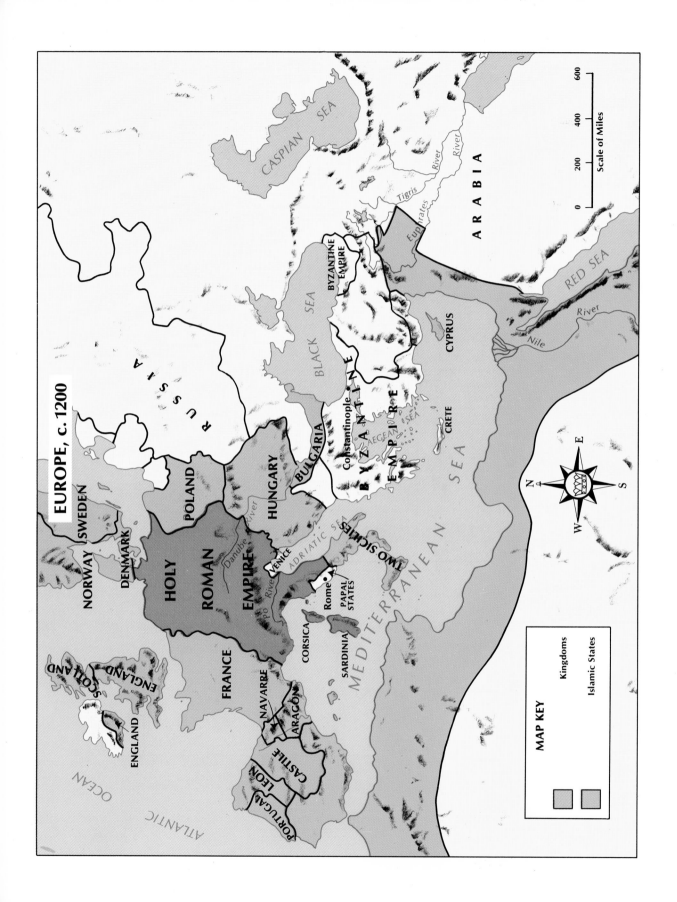

EUROPE, c. 1200

ATLANTIC OCEAN

SCOTLAND

ENGLAND

ENGLAND

NORWAY

SWEDEN

DENMARK

RUSSIA

POLAND

HOLY
ROMAN
EMPIRE

FRANCE

NAVARRE

ARAGON

LEÓN

CASTILE

PORTUGAL

CORSICA

SARDINIA

Po River

Danube River

VENICE

Rome

PAPAL STATES

TWO SICILIES

ADRIATIC SEA

HUNGARY

BULGARIA

BLACK SEA

CASPIAN SEA

BYZANTINE EMPIRE

Constantinople

B Y Z A N T I N E   E M P I R E

AEGEAN SEA

CRETE

CYPRUS

MEDITERRANEAN SEA

ARABIA

RED SEA

Nile River

Euphrates River

Tigris River

MAP KEY

Kingdoms

Islamic States

N E S W

600
400
200
0

Scale of Miles

ideas. This tension was already growing among the men of Latin Christendom. It was leading them to try out new ways of doing things. As their civilization grew stronger, they tried out many different forms of government.

The great lords did not want a strong government. They wanted to keep much of their power. The higher churchmen did not want a strong government, either. A strong government might interfere with the church. The churchmen wanted to have a weak empire. In such a government, the church could be the strongest power.

Many people, however, *did* want a strong government. The kings and their officials wanted to have a strong monarchy (mon′ ər kē). **Monarchy** means rule by one man—a monarch or king. Probably the knights and lesser lords wanted a strong monarchy too. It would check the power of the great lords.

The merchants also wanted a strong monarchy. To trade, they needed law and order. They thought that a monarchy would best be able to give it to them. Many town workers sided with the merchants in wanting a monarchy. In other places, merchants and townsmen wanted to have free city-states, like those of ancient Greece.

What the peasants wanted was not thought to be very important. They had no power or choice. If they had had power, they probably would have supported a monarch. That would have helped to check the power of the great lords in their region.

- Look at the diagram on page 111. This diagram shows how the different classes of medieval society wanted to be governed. Can you explain why each class preferred certain forms of government?

- Look at the map on page 112. Find the Holy Roman Empire. Most of this empire was where Germany is today. The Holy Roman Empire was not really strong. It was divided up and governed by hundreds of great nobles and dozens of free cities. How do you think it got the name it did?

- Notice how many kingdoms there were in Europe. Which of these medieval kingdoms are still nations? Name some modern nations of Europe whose names do not appear on the map.

A STRONG MONARCHY IN THE LATE MIDDLE AGES

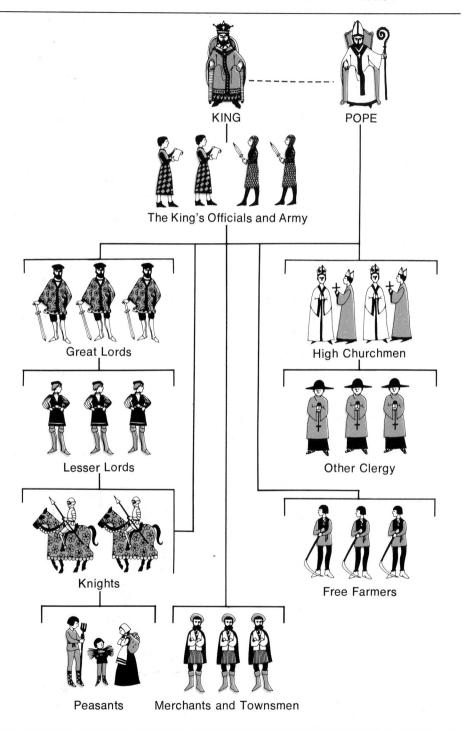

KING

POPE

The King's Officials and Army

Great Lords

High Churchmen

Lesser Lords

Other Clergy

Knights

Free Farmers

Peasants

Merchants and Townsmen

The Rise of Stronger Monarchies

In the end, monarchies turned out to be the strongest form of government in Latin Christendom. The monarch was called king or queen or prince. We still use the words *monarchy* or *kingdom* for this form of government.

Monarchs became stronger as the towns grew wealthier. With the help of townsmen, a king could raise enough taxes to pay for his own army. Gradually, he was able to take power away from the great nobles. The more power he had, the more he could gain. With power, he could make one set of laws for the whole kingdom. Peace and order, trade and prosperity grew under the national monarchies.

▶   Why would a king have to have his own army?

●   Why do you think people in the Middle Ages wanted to have a king rule them? Was there any other form of government that would really cut down the power of the great nobles?

The new strong monarchies were different from the older, feudal monarchies. Let us see some of the differences. Look at the diagram of the feudal system on page 77. This shows that a feudal king did not have much direct contact with different groups in society. The great lords stood between the king and the people. The king had very little freedom in raising taxes. He had little power to make laws.

Now compare this diagram with the one for a strong monarchy on page 114. In a strong monarchy, the king could have direct contact with many different groups in society. This gave him much greater freedom in raising taxes. The nobles might still refuse to grant him the taxes he asked for. The people, however, did not have much power to refuse. In a strong monarchy, the king was better able to make laws for all the people. He could expect all the people to give him their loyalty. They could not deny him their loyalty by giving it to a great noble instead.

●   Under the feudal system, to whom did the knights and peasants give their loyalty? As society advanced, do you think a strong monarchy would be a better form of government than the feudal system?

An artist in 1634 thought King Arthur and his Knights of the Round Table might have looked like this.

As the king's power grew, men and women began to think of themselves as members of a nation. The languages of Europe slowly took form. Men began to write in each of these languages. People who spoke and read the same language began to feel close to each other. People living in the land we call England began to say, "We are English." People living in the land we call France began to say, "We are French."

France and England were the strongest monarchies of Latin Christendom. In England, many stories were told about a king named Arthur. He was helped by his famous Knights of the Round Table.

People in the Middle Ages loved to tell stories about this legendary king. If King Arthur lived at all, he had lived centuries earlier—way back in the early part of the Dark Ages. In the stories, however, he was brought "up to date." When the people in the Middle Ages told about Arthur, they told much about themselves. They told about chivalry. They told about their ideas of a perfect king. They told how they thought a perfect king would treat his great lords.

★ Read some of the stories about King Arthur and his knights. How can you tell that the stories are "make believe"?

Rights and Parliaments

The strong monarchies arose out of a long struggle between the kings, the nobles, and the churchmen. Because of these other groups, a king in Latin Christendom could not be a dictator. He had to rule within the limits of the law. He had to respect the rights of certain groups in his kingdom.

The government headed by a king was based partly on Greek and Roman ideas. Among these were the ideas of the rule of law and of limited government. The government was also based on ideas that were new. These ideas arose out of the struggle between the kings, the nobles, and the churchmen. The ideas are still part of Western culture. The first one is: the people have rights that any ruler must recognize. The second one is: the people should be represented in the government.

The famous **Magna Carta** (Great Charter) of England is a good example of the first idea. It shows us how kings were forced to recognize the rights of the people. King John of England was a bad king. He lost wars with France. He attacked the church. He raised taxes whenever he felt like it. He used the law courts to get money. Soon all the powerful groups in England became very angry. The great nobles and the churchmen joined together. In 1215, they forced King John to sign a statement about the rights of Englishmen. After that time, the kings and queens of England had to promise to obey this great charter. The Magna Carta gave special rights to each group of citizens. The king had to respect the rights held by each group.

The Magna Carta had 63 paragraphs. Here are some of the rights that King John swore to respect.

> The Church of England should have its rights. It could choose its own bishops.

> The great nobles should have their rights. They would not be asked to pay more taxes to the king than they had paid in the past.

> If special taxes were needed, a council must vote. The council would be made up of the great nobles and clergy.

> The city of London should have its rights. So should other towns and cities.

> For a freeman to be put in jail or fined, two things were necessary. He must have broken the law of the land. He must have been tried by a jury.

The second new political idea that began in Latin Christendom was the idea of representative government. This means that the people should be represented in all matters that affect them. They should be represented especially when laws are changed and taxes are raised. To carry this out, the people must be able to choose men to represent them. The people's representatives can say what the people think, and can vote as the people would vote.

During the Middle Ages, representative government got its start in council meetings. The great nobles and the church leaders would go to the council meetings in person. The lesser nobles, the knights, and the townspeople were not allowed to go to the meetings in person. They were allowed to elect representatives to go in their place.

In England, such council meetings were called **parliaments** (pär' lə ments). Similar meetings were held in other national monarchies. As monarchs steadily gained power, some of them abolished these meetings. The English monarchs did not do this, however. The Parliament in England changed over the years, but it never disappeared. Centuries later, Americans studied the English Parliament. From it, they learned much about representative government.

This drawing of Parliament in 1295 is one of the earliest known.

We will read more about Latin Christendom in Chapter 8, which tells how medieval civilization began to change into modern Western civilization. Before going on, let us recall the questions we asked at the beginning of Chapter 4. How many of them can you answer now?

- What happened to Western Europe after the fall of Rome? What did people do to survive during this time?

- What did men do to bring civilization back? What inventions helped them?

► What was the culture of this new branch of civilization?

- What did the civilization of the Middle Ages pass on to modern Western civilization?

chapter 7

The Mongols of Mongolia

In our study of the Human Adventure we have learned about many civilized peoples. We have also learned about people who were not civilized. These people are called barbarians. Time after time, barbarians were a major cause of the ebbing of early civilizations. They lived on the fringes of the civilized world. They saw the good life of the civilized people. They wanted a share in this good life. Sometimes, the barbarians traded peacefully to get the things they wanted. More often, however, they did not. They attacked the civilized people and took what they wanted by force.

▶ What are the differences between barbarians and civilized people?

▶ Name some of the barbarians you have studied so far.

▶ What peoples did the Greeks consider barbarians? What peoples did the Chinese consider barbarians?

People in the early civilizations had good reason to fear the barbarians. In this chapter, we will find out about one group of barbarians. In some ways, it was quite a special group. It was the most frightening of all.

The story begins more than 700 years ago. A group of nomads were living in east central Asia. Like most barbarians, these nomads had never been united. They had always fought with outsiders. Yet they fought just as bitterly among themselves. Then suddenly, for a short time, they were united. In the thirteenth century, they fought as one nation. They became the most terrifying military force the world had ever known. They swept across Asia on horseback, conquering most of the continent. Quickly, they built the largest land empire in the history of the world.

These barbarians were the Mongols. Their conquest of civilized society was frightening. They tore down scores of great cities. They slaughtered hundreds of thousands of people. Civilized people lived in terror of them. Some believed that Mongols ate humans. Some believed that Mongol ponies were big enough to eat trees. It seemed that no story about the Mongols was too fantastic to believe.

How were the Mongols able to conquer civilized societies? How did it all begin? Let us try to answer these questions by looking at the Mongols and their homeland.

Mongols live in round tents called "yurts," which are made of wool felt stretched over wooden frames. The yurt can be taken down easily and set up again in another place.

The Land of the Mongols

A **steppe** (step) is land where short grasses grow. Across Asia lies a steppe that stretches for hundreds upon hundreds of miles. The poorest part of this vast area is Mongolia. Two-thirds of Mongolia is poor steppeland with a few mountain ranges. The other third is the great Gobi Desert. This desert is a barren, rocky area. It has little vegetation. Few people live on it.

Mongolia is a very dry land. It gets little rain. Moist air coming from the Indian Ocean is blocked by high mountains to the south. Temperatures in Mongolia run to extremes. The summers are short and very hot. The winters are long and bitterly cold. There are few trees and valleys to provide shelter from the winter blizzards. Mongolia is one of the world's least attractive places to live. Find the steppeland on the map on page 124. Find the Gobi Desert. From what you have just read, see if you can locate the area where the Mongols were living.

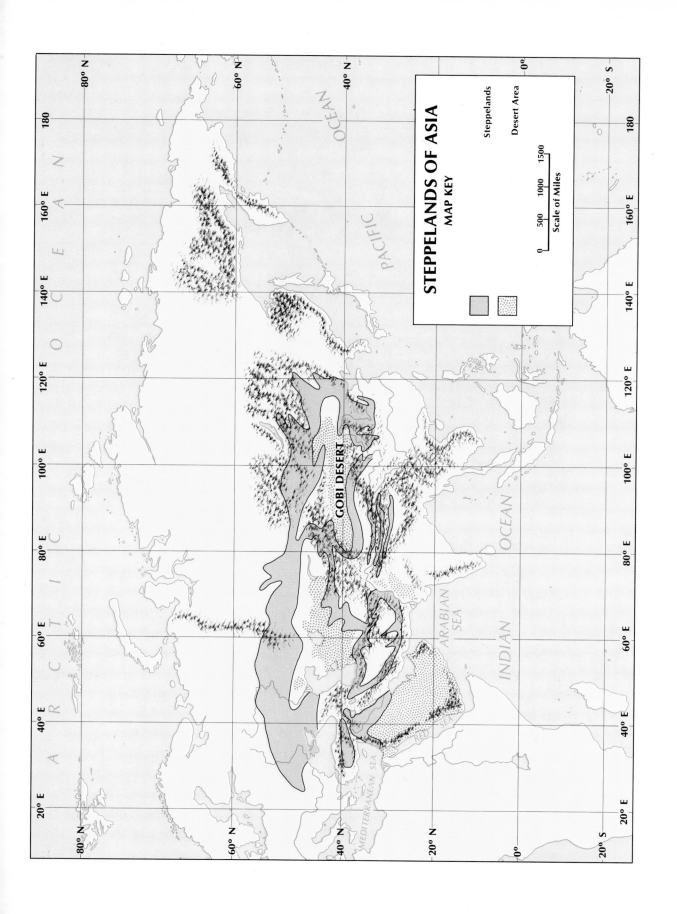

STEPPELANDS OF ASIA
MAP KEY

Steppelands

Desert Area

Scale of Miles

0   500   1000   1500

GOBI DESERT

The land of Mongolia has always been poor. The population has always been scattered. Yet, men have lived in Mongolia for thousands of years. They have had to be tough. The early Mongols had to develop a way of life that would let them survive. This way of life did not have the marks of a civilized culture. The Mongols did not settle in one place and farm the land. They did not build cities or make permanent homes. Instead, they followed a nomadic way of life. They always moved from place to place with all their belongings.

- Which way of life needs more land to support people — nomadic life or civilized life? Why?

▶ Do you think that the land and climate of Mongolia would produce a gentle way of life or a tough way of life? Why?

The Childhood of Temujin

Into this fierce and restless land was born one of the greatest military leaders of all time. Let us read about him.

In the year 1162, a boy was born to the chief of the Yakka Mongols. The baby was named Temujin (tem'ə jin). His name meant "iron."

Temujin's father was not in camp the day his son was born. He was off raiding another tribe. That was a perfectly normal thing for a Mongol man to be doing.

Mongol children grew up quickly. Temujin learned the ways of men at an early age. He was one of the best wrestlers in his tribe. Wrestling was popular among Mongol boys. It was a very rough sport. Bones were often broken during wrestling matches. For several hours every day, Temujin practiced shooting his bow and arrow.

Temujin spent a great deal of time riding his pony. He wanted to become an expert horseman like his father. Temujin loved to take his pony out for a race. Sometimes he and his friends would race as far as 50 miles.

- Did Temujin have an education? What was the aim of a Mongol education?

Temujin Becomes Head of His Family

When Temujin was 13, tragedy struck his family. His father, chief of the Yakka Mongols, lay dying. He had probably been poisoned by members of another tribe. His last words were, "Bring Temujin to me." Temujin raced to his side. His father was dead before he reached him.

A new chief had to be found for the tribe. As the oldest son, Temujin inherited his father's tents and herds. However, he was only 13. He was too young to be chief. The tribe could not agree on a new chief. They decided to break up. Each family would try to join another tribe that already had a strong chief. As chief, Temujin's father had made many enemies. Now that he was dead, his enemies would surely seek revenge.

Temujin did not want to join another tribe. He decided to stay where he was. He tried to convince other families to stay, too. They would not listen. They deserted the family of the dead chief. Temujin's mother and her seven children were left alone. For many years they had to live as outcasts. They kept on the move, knowing that their enemies would never stop looking for them.

- Why do you suppose a strong family head was so important to the Mongol family? Why was a strong chief so important to the Mongol tribe?

Temujin's Idea of Uniting the Mongols

As Temujin grew to manhood, he began to think of organizing the Mongols into a single, united people. He wanted them to give their highest loyalty to an idea. He wanted the idea of unity to become important to the Mongols. He wanted it to become more important than their loyalty to family and tribe. Temujin began to build up a band of loyal followers. Among Temujin's followers, honor and loyalty to the leader became almost sacred.

- What loyalties do we have in our society? Do we owe allegiance to a group that is bigger than the family? Explain.

- Who united the Arabs? How did he do it?

Temujin Becomes Chief of the Mongols

Temujin became known among the Mongol tribes as skillful and fearless. More and more people flocked to him. They began to see advantages in joining together under his name. They would be protected against enemy tribes. They would also be able to fight people in other lands. Then great riches would be theirs.

By the year 1200, Temujin had a following of 100,000 Mongol families. Within a few years, he had succeeded in uniting all of Mongolia. United, the Mongols went on to conquer many of the Turkish tribes west of Mongolia. By 1206, all of the Mongol tribes had pledged undying loyalty to Temujin. As the chief of all Mongols, he was given a new name. It was Genghis Khan (jeng'gis kän'), which means "perfect warrior."

An expert Mongol horseman uses a long pole to round up a herd of horses.

● Now that the barbarians of Mongolia were united, what might that mean to civilized peoples?

● A personal leader is one who inspires strong feelings of personal loyalty among his people. Was Temujin a personal leader of his people? Can you name some personal leaders in the world today? Can you name some from other cultures you have studied?

The Mongol Army

Genghis organized his warriors into an army. Later, there were several Mongol armies. Each army was divided into units. Each unit had a leader. With this organization, it was easier for Genghis to find out what was going on in the Mongol armies. He had to ask only a few leaders. Genghis, of course, was the supreme leader of all the armies. No one disobeyed his commands.

The Mongol armies were organized to travel fast and far. Each warrior was able to "live off the land" as the army marched. A warrior did not have to depend on supplies from home. He took whatever supplies he needed—or wanted.

A section of the Great Wall in China

The Mongols Invade China

To the east and south of Mongolia lay the mighty Chinese Empire. Genghis had never been to China. Still, he knew a lot about it. He decided to invade it. There seemed to be enough booty in the empire to make every Mongol warrior a rich man.

To the Chinese, the Mongols were barbarians. The Chinese looked down on all barbarians. They thought that barbarians were not fit to share in civilized life. Centuries earlier, the Chinese had built a Great Wall to keep barbarian invaders out of their country. The Great Wall was more than 1,500 miles long. It was about twenty feet high. That made it too high for a horse to jump over. It was so wide that six men could march side by side on top of it. Small groups of Chinese soldiers were stationed every few miles along the wall. From these places, they could easily spot trouble. Then they could rush soldiers to the point of attack.

Because of the Great Wall, a few Chinese defenders could defeat a large force of barbarians. The wall had held off many barbarian raids. Could it hold off a full-scale barbarian invasion? China was soon to find out.

▶ Did the Chinese have more to fear before or after the Mongols were united under Genghis Khan?

● How do you suppose the barbarians felt about the Great Wall of China? Why?

The Chinese outnumbered the Mongols 50 to 1. However, most Chinese men were peasants and city dwellers. Very few were warriors. Yet every Mongol man and teenage boy was an expert warrior. That was their only task in life. The Mongol herds did not need care. Mongol women and children could handle things at home. The Mongol men were free to make war. They knew how to do almost nothing else.

Genghis and his horsemen used trickery to pass through the Great Wall. The Chinese knew that Genghis and his warriors were coming. They sent armies to try to stop the Mongols before they got to the wall. Genghis was clever and thought that this might happen. Therefore, he sent part of his army a different way to trick the Chinese. The Chinese fell for this trick and followed that part of the Mongol army. Then Genghis and the rest of his warriors were able to cross the Great Wall.

Soon, however, Genghis faced problems that were new to him. China had many great cities. These cities were surrounded by high walls. They could hold out for months. How could Genghis take these cities?

Genghis was able to learn new ideas from Chinese prisoners. These prisoners told him about the art of **siege warfare**. In this type of warfare, an army surrounds an enemy city. The army cuts off the city from food supplies. The people begin to starve. In the end, they have to surrender. Genghis also learned how to make

*In this old painting, the Mongols attack a city.
Their leader watches from a bridge.*

The Mongols loved to tell stories about Genghis Khan. In one story they said that he once told some Muslims that he had been sent to conquer them in punishment for their sins. Here he is shown speaking to them from a richly decorated pulpit.

battering rams to break down the gates of a city. He learned how to use catapults (kat'ə pults), which are machines that throw large rocks. Genghis even learned how to use gunpowder to blow up walls. He combined all these new weapons with the old Mongol ways of fighting. The Chinese cities began to fall.

Taking Advantage of Civilization

By 1214, Genghis had conquered all of China north of the Yellow River. What would he do with the conquered land? He did not trust the civilized way of life. To Genghis, only Chinese booty was worthwhile. He was destroying China simply to get booty.

One day, Genghis met a Chinese scholar who told him about another way to profit from his conquests. The scholar explained the system of tribute. Tribute was a kind of tax. The Chinese could be made to pay tribute to the Mongols. Each year they would give the Mongols money or goods. If they failed to pay, Genghis could punish them. Tribute was better than booty. It came year after year, but booty came only once.

Genghis was pleased with the scholar's advice. He made him a trusted adviser. In time, the scholar became the greatest statesman of the Mongol Empire. He probably saved a great many lives by showing Genghis how to take advantage of civilization without destroying it.

- Do you think the Chinese scholar was a traitor to his people? Why or why not?

- Why was it so hard for Genghis to see any value in civilization once he had stripped it of booty? Do you agree with him? Explain.

After conquering China, Genghis went back to Mongolia. He did not care that the wealth of China was at his command. He chose to live in the old Mongol way. He ate the same food and wore the same clothes as before.

Genghis wanted his people to live in the same way that he did. If the Mongols settled down in cities, he thought they would be weakened. Sooner or later, the Mongols' way of life would be destroyed. Genghis did not want that to happen. Still, he also wanted them to have some of the good things of civilization.

Now these things would come to them in tribute. This flow of Chinese wealth continued throughout Genghis' life. It continued throughout the lives of his sons and grandsons.

- Do you think Genghis was right in fearing that civilized life would destroy his armies? Explain.

- Did the Mongols become civilized after conquering the civilization of China? What happened to other barbarians you have studied? What happened to the Arabs when they ruled an empire? Were the Mongols unusual? Explain.

The Mongols depended greatly upon expert horsemanship for their military victories. Here their unfortunate prisoners are shown being led off by the Mongolian cavalry.

Genghis Looks West

A few years after conquering China, Genghis became curious about the lands to the west. He wondered about the glittering cities of Islam. The Shah Muhammad ruled over Persia (now Iran), Afghanistan, part of northern India, and a large part of southern Russia. Genghis sent a messenger to this shah. He offered him trade. The shah accepted the khan's offer.

● Why do you suppose Genghis wanted trade instead of conquest? What might he have learned about civilization?

The Mongols prepared a great caravan of 500 camels. They sent it off to the shah, loaded with treasure. Along the way, one of the shah's governors robbed the caravan. He killed its members. Genghis was furious. He demanded that the governor be turned over to him. The shah refused.

Genghis prepared for war. It was a long way to the lands of the Shah Muhammad. The Mongols had to cross 2,000 miles of mountains and deserts. As they marched, the whole front part of the Mongol army spread across about 1,000 miles. The shah could not tell where the Mongols would strike first.

Within two years, Genghis had destroyed the shah's lands. The Mongol armies did not stop until they reached Eastern Europe. The Mongols were then masters of an enormous empire. As you can see on the map on page 137, it stretched from the Pacific Ocean to the Caspian Sea.

In 1227, Genghis Khan died. In all his years as leader of the Mongols, he never knew defeat. He had made himself the most powerful man in the world. He was also the most feared, and probably the most hated.

● Can you compare Genghis Khan with any other conquerors? Explain.

The Successors of Genghis Khan

After the death of Genghis, his son Ogdai (og'dī) became khan. Under Ogdai, a second wave of Mongol conquests began. Mongol armies sacked and destroyed the cities of southern China. They captured Korea, a small country close to China. In the west,

Left, Genghis Khan (1167–1227). Right, his grandson, Kublai Khan (1216–1294).

the Mongols pushed into Russia and Eastern Europe. They defeated the knights of Poland, Hungary, and Germany. One after another, European armies were turned back by the Mongols.

Western Europe was barely saved from Mongol invasion. In 1241, Ogdai Khan died. A new khan had to be chosen. To the Mongols, that was important business. A conquest could be made any time. At least, that is what they had come to think. The Mongols withdrew from Europe and never returned.

● Why do you think European knights were defeated by Mongol horsemen?

After Ogdai's death, the Mongols had a number of khans. None of them became very strong leaders, but they did continue the Mongol conquests. They conquered lands in the Middle East. The last great khan was elected in 1260. He was Kublai (kü′ blī) Khan, the nephew of Ogdai. Kublai had been only a boy when his grandfather, the great Genghis, died. Kublai had been taught by Chinese scholars and had learned the arts of civilization. He was more interested in ruling than in destroying. The reign of Kublai Khan (1260–1294) was the golden age of the Mongol Empire. Kublai Khan moved his capital from Mongolia to

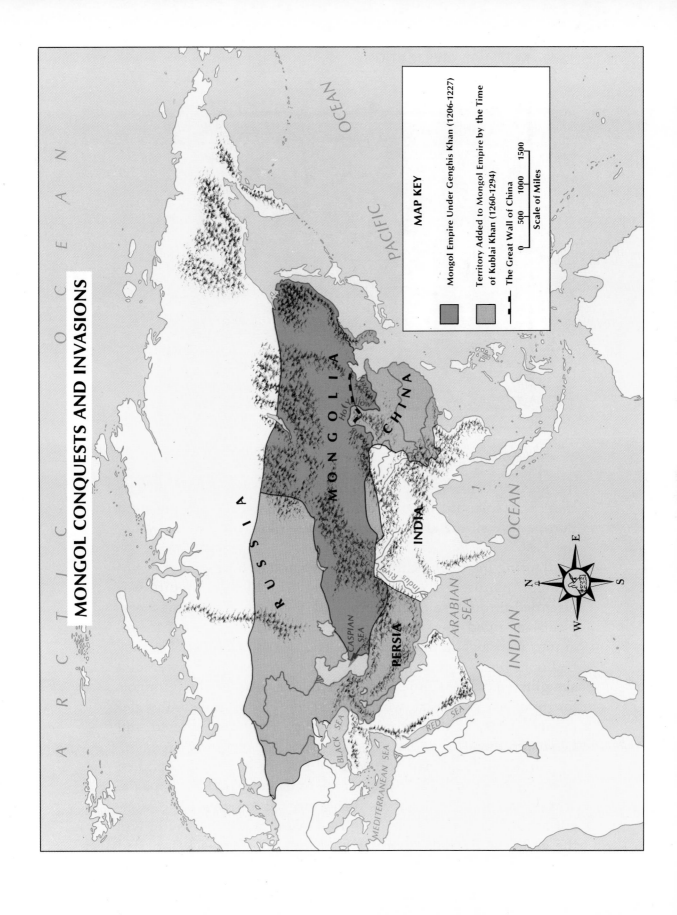

MONGOL CONQUESTS AND INVASIONS

MAP KEY

Mongol Empire Under Genghis Khan (1206-1227)

Territory Added to Mongol Empire by the Time
of Kublai Khan (1260-1294)

The Great Wall of China

Scale of Miles

0   500   1000   1500

ARCTIC OCEAN

PACIFIC OCEAN

INDIAN OCEAN

RUSSIA

MONGOLIA

CHINA

INDIA

PERSIA

CASPIAN SEA

BLACK SEA

MEDITERRANEAN SEA

RED SEA

ARABIAN SEA

Indus River

N E S W

Marco Polo traveled from Venice to the court of Kublai Khan.

the ancient Chinese city of Peking. He built great palaces. His court was splendid beyond comparison. Marco Polo came from Europe to visit the khan's court. He described it as "the jewel of the East."

During his reign, Kublai Khan began the third great wave of Mongol conquest. It was also the last. The Mongol Empire was extended through southern China. By then it was the largest empire ever ruled by a single person. Yet the victorious Mongol armies were beginning to change. They were not as cruel as they had once been. Sometimes the people in defeated cities were not slaughtered. One Chinese city held out against the Mongols for five years. Kublai was impressed. He promised the defenders safety if they would surrender. They surrendered and he spared them!

Under Kublai Khan, the Mongol Empire had finally reached its limit. Perhaps it was just too large to be governed. Perhaps the armies had to cover distances that were just too great. The Mongol armies tried to invade countries in the west, the south, and the east. The defending armies held them off. Never before had this happened! Still, when Kublai Khan died in 1294, the Mongol Empire stretched from the Pacific Ocean to the Black Sea. Look at the map on page 137 to compare the size of the empire under Genghis Khan and Kublai Khan.

What had happened to change the Mongols at the height of their power? They had been affected by civilization, just as Genghis had feared. The highest leader of the Mongols had become civilized. Mongol warriors were settling down into comfortable, civilized ways. As Genghis had feared, the Mongols were becoming like the people they conquered. They were no longer the terrible warriors whom Genghis had led out of the Mongolian steppe.

After Kublai Khan died, no other great khans appeared. Mongol power collapsed almost as quickly as it had arisen. From then on, life on the Mongolian steppe continued as it had been before. Even today, most Mongols are nomads tending their flocks.

The Legacy of the Mongols

Genghis Khan and his successors left a trail of terrible destruction behind them. No one will ever know how many lives were lost. No one will ever know how many beautiful things were destroyed. We do know that the cost to civilized countries was enormous. The countries of the Middle East never fully recovered from the brutal Mongol conquest. As a result of the Mongol occupation, the growth of China was slowed. Western Europe was spared only by Ogdai Khan's death.

The Mongols could not add anything of their own to the Human Adventure. Still, they changed the course of history. They brought the civilizations of the East and West closer together. Genghis Khan, the great destroyer, broke down the barriers between civilizations. He forced the civilizations into contact with each other. Western Europe, in particular, was to benefit from this contact. China was forced to share some of its rich culture with other peoples. From China, gunpowder, printing, and the compass came to Western Europe. Such important inventions helped Western Europe to gain a lead over other civilizations.

This map of the world was drawn by a European between 1452 and 1458.

chapter 8

The Rise of Western Europe

By 1400, there were four especially important branches of civilization in the world. They were China, India, Islam, and Latin Christendom. From our reading, we know that no one branch of civilization had ever dominated the world in earlier times. But something entirely new was about to happen in the Human Adventure. One of these four was about to take the lead. Latin Christendom was about to develop into the civilization of Western Europe.

▶ What three continents made up the Old World in 1400? What is the name of the landmass that is made up of *two* continents?

Western Europe About To Expand

Suppose we could ask a clever man living in 1400 to play a guessing game. We would ask him to guess which branch of civiliza-

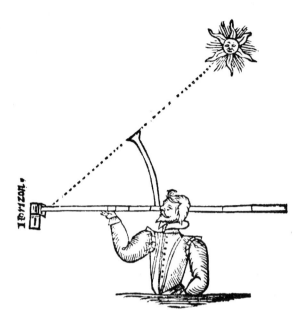

This seaman demonstrates the use of a backstaff, one of the instruments developed in the sixteenth century to help sailors determine their ship's position.

tion was about to become the most powerful. Which branch would he guess? Being a clever man, he would want to consider the question from several points of view.

Our friend might begin by taking the geographer's point of view. He would think about the locations of the four branches of civilization. He would remember that China, India, and Latin Christendom were out on the edges of the civilized world. He would know that Islam was at the very center. Besides, he would remember that Islam covered more territory than any of the other three. From the geographer's point of view, then, he would guess—Islam!

Then our friend might take the economist's point of view. He would say that Islam had another great advantage. It was the gateway to Africa, Asia, and Europe. It had favorable trade routes and a prosperous trade. From the economist's point of view, then, he would guess—Islam again!

Last, our friend might take the historian's point of view. He would think about long traditions of government under the rule of law. He would remember that only two branches of civilization had such traditions. Those two were China and Islam. Putting this together with the other points of view, our friend would not hesitate. He would guess—Islam, for sure!

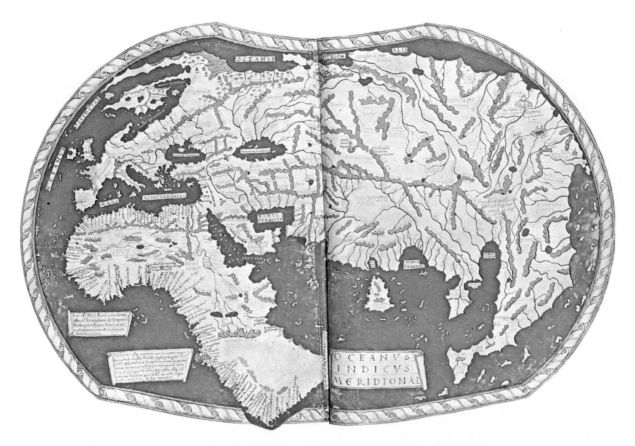

A tremendous amount of exploration took place after 1450. Notice in particular how much more is known about the west coast of Africa on this map drawn near the end of the fifteenth century than on the earlier map on page 140.

As we know, our clever friend would be wrong. Suppose we could ask him the very same question a hundred years later, in 1500. Then he might give the right answer. During the fifteenth century, Latin Christendom began to change and expand. Its people sailed away from Western Europe in their ships. They found new seaways to the East. They even discovered a "new world." Western Europe began to influence other parts of the world quickly and strongly. The result was almost like an explosion.

Why did Western Europe begin to "explode"? We will see that the answer to that question has many parts. The Western Europeans were eager to change. The church became separated from the government, and this gave the people more freedom to change. They had advantages in natural environment. They gained important political and economic advantages.

SOME FORCES MAKING FOR CHANGE IN WESTERN EUROPE, c. 1400

1. The tension between Judeo-Christian and Greco-Roman ideas

2. New ideas from Islam and China and India

3. New learning from Greek and Roman books

4. Strong monarchies and patriotism

5. The tension between Church and State

6. The natural environment, physical features and location of Western Europe

7. Growth of trade and wealth and towns

اسرخأفلخبررةثمراعك حتی كلا بنتی منه شئ وان أردن
جعله اوصه فلح ناخ ناح امض ترشه فی الشمس الحار
فانه يكون أبيض بالغ وجزقه انناخذ نفه جدك قدقه
ونفرشه عليها فی بربه وهی علم جمر ثم حركه فاذا رأيت لونه
مثل الرماد فار فعه وبرده وهو نعسا مثل غسل القد به طبيعته

This Arabic manuscript discusses the preparation of certain medicines.

An Eagerness To Change

In 1400, the people of Latin Christendom, or Western Europe, were eager to learn. From older civilizations, they gained new knowledge and skills. As they came to know other cultures, they adopted new and different ways of thinking and doing things.

It is the old story that we have seen so often in the Human Adventure. People use ideas from older civilizations to change their own. A new civilization is the result. The Greeks took ideas from the Middle Eastern civilizations. The Arabs took ideas from the Persians and the Greeks. The people of Latin Christendom had taken ideas from Islam and from ancient Greece and Rome.

Western Europe was a "young" civilization. It was more willing to change than most "young" civilizations had been. It was ready to copy and experiment.

The Western Europeans had inherited Greco-Roman ideas and Judeo-Christian ideas. Both sets of ideas were part of their **heritage**, or tradition. During the Middle Ages, they had lived mainly on the Judeo-Christian part of their heritage. During the next few centuries, they rediscovered the Greco-Roman part of their heritage. They read manuscripts that had been written by the ancient Greeks and Romans. They studied ancient statues and architecture.

Historians have given this movement a special name. They call it the revival of learning, or the **Renaissance** (ren'ə säns'). Renaissance is a French word that means "rebirth." During the Renaissance, the learning and culture of Greece and Rome were "born again."

However, this revival of learning soon led to a feeling of tension. The Western Europeans felt the pull of the two powerful sets of controlling ideas. They could now think of more than one answer to the important questions of life. Sometimes the answers did not agree with each other. This made the Western Europeans restless, but it also made them excited. Now they wanted to find answers of their own. They were eager to find new and different ways of doing things.

- What were these two sets of controlling ideas? Why were they partly opposed to each other? How do you think this tension, or pull, might have affected the way in which Western Europeans thought and acted?

- Would a Confucian Chinese have been torn between two sets of controlling ideas? Were the Chinese interested in borrowing ideas from other cultures? Were they eager to change and experiment? Were they eager to invent things? Explain.

- Why were the Arabs willing to learn and experiment in the early centuries of Islam? Why did they gradually lose their interest in experimenting?

RENAISSANCE ART

A Lady with a Pearl Necklace
School of the Romagna, Italy

Madonna and Child
Filippo Lippi

Madonna in the Clouds
Donatello (1386–1466)

CONTRIBUTIONS OF OTHER CIVILIZATIONS TO
WESTERN EUROPEAN CIVILIZATION

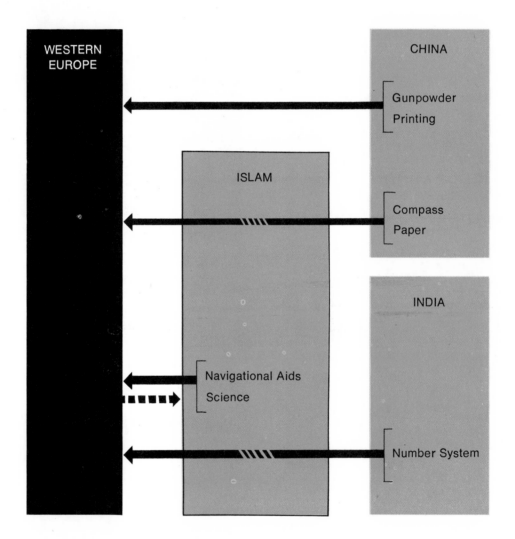

A Feeling of Strength and Security

The rise of Western Europe was aided by the strong faith of the people. The men and women of Latin Christendom believed that Christianity was the only true religion. The church leaders told them — and they believed — that Christianity should grow. It ought to be the religion of all the people in the world. They believed that people were wrong who did not do as Christians did.

This faith gave the people confidence. They gained confidence from their armies, too. Their armies had become strong because they were needed to protect Western Europe. They remained strong for another reason. The Western Europeans kept on fighting among themselves. Sometimes they were violent and cruel.

- What examples can you give of the warlike nature of the men of Latin Christendom? Can you give any examples of their cruelty? Can you give any examples of their peaceful nature? Explain.

The Crusades are a good example of how confident the Western Europeans were. During the Crusades, the power of Latin Christendom began to turn outward. The Crusades brought Western Europeans into closer contact with other branches of civilization. This helped to bring about a growth of trade. As a result of the Crusades, more foreign ideas and foreign products came into Western Europe. The Western Europeans were not afraid to adopt any ideas or products that might be useful.

- Look at the chart on page 148. What did Europeans learn from China, from India, and from Islam? What do you think the dashed line from Western Europe to Islam means?

Church and State in Western Europe

There was another important cause of change in Western Europe. In this culture, the church was separated from the government. This separation helped men to be free to think and to experiment. Such freedom did not come all at once. There were times when the church joined with the kings and great nobles. Together, these groups forced all people to think in the same way. Some-

The architecture of these cathedrals reflects the power and vitality of the medieval church. Left, Notre Dame in Paris; below left, Cologne cathedral in Germany; below right, Chartres cathedral. Even in the sixteenth century, great monuments such as St. Peter's in Rome, opposite page, were being built.

times, however, church leaders disagreed with the government. They did not think that force was the right way to change people. They said that religious authority was quite different from political power.

By the end of the Middle Ages, the church leaders knew that the church must stand by itself. It could not depend on the power of kings. From that time on, the idea of separating the church from the government was well established.

Little by little, freedom to think and choose and experiment grew stronger in Western Europe. Religious freedom, in the end, helped men and women to think for themselves. When people think for themselves, they may be ready for new ideas and changes.

▶ Which was oldest in Latin Christendom—the church or the kingdoms of France or England? Which was the oldest in the Byzantine Empire—the empire or the Greek Orthodox Church? In which part of Christendom—Eastern or Western—was the church more likely to be independent of the state?

● Why do you think Latin Christendom became known as Western Europe? Explain.

Advantages of the Natural Environment

The Western Europeans enjoyed other kinds of advantages as well. Some of these advantages were geographical. Western Europe had many natural resources. It had an abundance of ores, especially iron. It had large amounts of timber and building stone. There were broad, fertile plains where a surplus of food could be grown. There were many rivers that could provide power.

- What kinds of things did Europeans make with their ores, timber, stone, and other resources?

- What agricultural improvement helped the peasants of Western Europe to grow a surplus of food? What effects did a surplus of food have on Western European society?

The most important geographical advantage of Western Europe was its shape and location. Much of the land is formed into peninsulas. No spot is very far from the sea. The sea provides routes for trade. The deep rivers of Western Europe are wide enough for trading ships and boats. Western Europeans began sailing the seas and trading just as the Greeks and Romans had done. There was one great difference, however. The great Atlantic Ocean is much rougher than the Mediterranean Sea. That is why the Western Europeans had to build stronger ships than the Greeks built. That is why the Western Europeans had to become superb seamen.

- ★ Find a map of Western Europe in an atlas. Locate the peninsulas of Scandinavia, Denmark, Spain, and Italy. Locate the rivers Elbe, Rhine, Seine, Thames, Loire, Garonne, Tagus, Rhone, and Po. Locate the Baltic Sea.

- Carrying goods by water is much cheaper than carrying them overland. Almost all Europeans are close to at least one navigable body of water. How would these two facts affect life in Europe? Could small, lightweight, luxury goods be traded? Could heavy things, like grain and wine and building materials, be traded?

- After the discovery of the New World, was Western Europe still "on the fringe" of the known world? Explain.

This drawing of one of his ships was included in a letter written by Columbus on February 14, 1493, during his return voyage from the New World.

Political Life and Growth

We have read that in the later Middle Ages, the people of Western Europe were beginning to form nations. One group was beginning to think of itself as French. Another group was beginning to think of itself as English. The same thing was happening everywhere. People were beginning to feel proud of their nation. They were beginning to love it. They were becoming **patriotic**. Patriotic men want to serve their nation. They want to improve their society. They feel responsible for their country. They want to share in its government.

The strong monarchies helped these patriotic ideas to grow. When kings needed to raise taxes or make new laws, they had to get help. They had to go to the powerful groups in society. They called together parliaments. The great nobles, the churchmen, the knights, and the townsmen all came to these parliaments. They all shared in the government of their nation.

Gold coins such as these from Spain played an important part in the developing economies of medieval Europe.

By sharing in the government, these men helped to make their nations more active. This could not have happened unless the nations had had powerful groups to share in the government. The new nations had many eager, free men who were ready for change. Such men were like the patriotic citizens of Athens or early Rome. However, the new nations were much larger than any city-state had been. They contained many more people. They had far greater wealth.

- Name some societies you have studied that had no powerful groups to share in the government.

Economic Life and Growth

The spirit of change could be seen in the economic life of Western Europe, too. During the Dark Ages, men had lived in a *subsistence economy*. They had produced just enough to stay alive. Money had almost vanished. Trade had almost disappeared. Each manor had produced just enough goods for its own peasant farmers and knights. During and after the twelfth century, however, this changed.

- Review the changes in economic life that led to the rise of civilization in Christendom. (Consider: surplus products, division of labor, trade, towns, money, capital.)

"Explosive" economic changes began to take place in Western Europe. Traders were bringing goods and ideas from faraway places in Asia. The Crusades were expanding trade with the Middle East. Beyond the Middle East were China and India. A few Europeans, like Marco Polo, visited these faraway civilizations.

The rich people of Latin Christendom wanted to buy fine goods from Asia. They wanted spices, like pepper and cloves. They wanted cloths, like silk and cotton. They wanted precious jewels. They wanted fine china cups and plates. Asian merchants brought these goods to the ports of the eastern Mediterranean. There they sold the goods to European merchants. The European merchants brought them back to Western Europe. From such trade, the merchants made large profits. Because of these profits, some towns turned into wealthy cities.

- Find a map of Asia in an atlas. Suppose you were an Arab merchant. What land routes might you use to bring silk from China to Syria? What sea route would you use from India to Egypt?

- Now find a map of Europe. The first wealthy trading cities of Western Europe were in Italy. Locate Venice, Genoa, and Florence. How did their locations help them?

- How would goods get from Venice or Genoa to France or England?

- What goods might the merchants of Western Europe trade for Asian products? What bulky goods would the Western European people trade among themselves?

The merchants had to keep track of the many goods bought and sold. They had to keep records of the money taken in and paid out. They began to develop better ways of doing business. During the fifteenth century, Italian merchants began to use Hindu-Arabic numerals to keep their records. To do their figuring, they began to use the kind of arithmetic we use today.

- Why do you think the Italian merchants were the first Europeans to use Hindu-Arabic numerals?

- Why would it be easier for the merchants to figure with Hindu-Arabic numerals than with older methods?

Once a merchant started to make large profits, he could turn part of his profits into savings or capital. He could buy more ships. He could hire more workers. He could lend capital to a man who wanted to start a business. He could lend capital to a landlord or farmer who needed to borrow money until harvest time. This is how the **banking system** of Western Europe began.

★ Make sure you know the meaning of *profit, capital, lending, borrowing, loan,* and *bank.*

● When money is borrowed from a merchant or a bank, how does the borrower pay for the use of the money? What is the meaning of *interest*? What is the difference between *profit* and *interest*?

● The profits from trade and manufacturing were often bigger and were gained faster than those from agriculture. Can you see how this would make the merchants and townsmen as powerful as the great nobles? Might merchants and townsmen become more powerful than the nobles? Explain.

A Money-and-Market Economy

The bankers were a great help to trade. They set up branches of banks in the Western European cities. They even set up branches in some Muslim cities. From then on, a merchant did not need to carry large amounts of money with him. Instead, he would place his money in one branch of a bank. The bank would give him a letter of credit. The merchant could use this letter of credit at any other branch of the bank. He could use it to take money out of a bank that was hundreds of miles away. He could send it to pay a foreign merchant for goods.

● What services do banks perform today? Do they give letters of credit? Is a letter of credit the same as a bank check? Is a letter of credit the same as a credit card? How does a bank make a profit?

● See if you can explain how the banks helped producers as well as traders. (Think: How could a man get capital to buy tools and a workshop in order to make goods?)

A medieval moneychanger and his wife weigh out gold coins.

The economic life of Western Europe kept changing. In one country after another, the feudal economy began to disappear. In its place came the **money-and-market economy**. This is an economy based on capital and investment. Little by little, peasants were freed from being bound to their lord's land. Some peasants became workers and traders in the towns. Some became wage earners on farms. Others became tenant farmers or bought small farms of their own. All this happened slowly. By 1400, however, the process was underway.

All these economic changes encouraged men to invent things. Many of the inventions led to further inventions. Many of these inventions would help the Western Europeans to explore their world. For the first time, people from one part of the civilized world were able to learn about every other part of the world. The result was an exciting age of exploration and expansion.

Nuns stand in front of a modern chapel in Ronchamps, France.

conclusion

The Continuing
Ebb and Flow
of Civilization

When we first began our study of the Human Adventure, we started on a voyage of discovery.

We went back thousands of years to the time when civilization was just beginning. We traveled far away from our own country to Mesopotamia, the land where civilization began. The Sumerians of Mesopotamia were the first civilized people. Their culture was different from that of any people who had lived before them. The Sumerians made changes in many ways of doing things. These changes affected the way of life of people who lived after them.

● What changes did the Sumerians make in agriculture and in the production of goods? What changes did they make in trade, religion, government and laws, and social life?

The civilization of Sumer lasted about 1,500 years. When Sumer disappeared, it was forgotten for a long time. New

159

branches of civilization arose. Some were in Mesopotamia, and some were in other river valleys.

By the sixth century B.C., important civilizations had arisen in places far away from one another. The people of each of these civilizations had a different way of life. They had different controlling ideas and different cultures.

▶ Review the meaning of *culture* and *controlling ideas*.

● What were the important controlling ideas of the cultures in China, India, Palestine, and Greece around 600–500 B.C.? Which of these ideas have had the greatest influence on our own Western civilization?

In China and India, civilization lasted. Around the Mediterranean, however, many changes were taking place. Several great branches of civilization rose and fell.

The Roman Empire was at its height during the first century A.D. Much of the land conquered earlier by Alexander the Great had become part of this empire. By the eighth century A.D.—long after the Roman Empire had fallen—another great civilization had been formed. This was the Islamic, or Muslim, Empire. At its height, the Islamic Empire controlled the land to the east, west, and south of the Mediterranean Sea. Look at the three maps on page 161 that show the Mediterranean area under Alexander, the Romans, and the Muslims.

▶ What part of Alexander's empire did not become part of the Roman Empire? What lands outside Alexander's empire became part of the Roman Empire?

▶ What lands of the Roman Empire became part of the Islamic Empire? What lands did not?

In this part of *The Human Adventure,* we have studied four very different civilizations and cultures—those of Islam, medieval Africa, Latin Christendom, and the Mongol Empire. We have seen how some of the barbarians and primitive peoples advanced toward civilization. They were eager to learn. They were willing to borrow the ideas of older cultures. Sometimes they were driven by a forceful idea of their own.

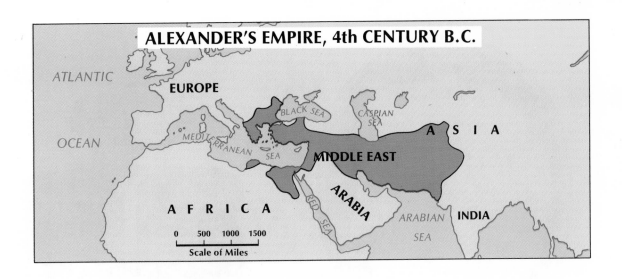

ALEXANDER'S EMPIRE, 4th CENTURY B.C.

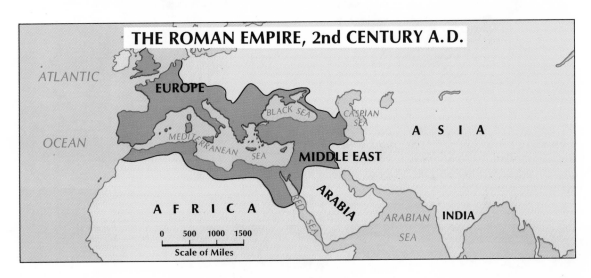

THE ROMAN EMPIRE, 2nd CENTURY A.D.

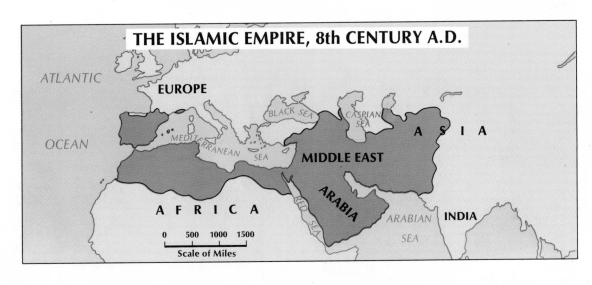

THE ISLAMIC EMPIRE, 8th CENTURY A.D.

These four photographs represent some of the surviving accomplishments of civilizations that flourished before medieval times. Upper left, a Roman cameo of Augustus Caesar; upper right, a Hebrew tablet, symbol of the Ten Commandments; below, a Sumerian couple from 2500 B.C.; opposite page, the Egyptian temple at Karnak.

We have also seen how some civilizations flourished and began to decline. The controlling idea that gave rise to the Islamic Empire also helped to destroy it in the end. The great African kingdoms were destroyed by attacks. The Mongols built a great empire but could not build a civilization. After all their brutal conquests, their empire collapsed as suddenly as it had arisen.

We have seen that the civilization of Western Europe got off to a late start. It was built by rival groups of barbarian invaders. However, these barbarians were eager to become civilized. They borrowed ideas from the past. They borrowed ideas from civilizations that were still existing in other parts of the world.

In 1500, the Human Adventure was entering a new stage. Many different cultures were about to come into contact with one another. Western European civilization was about to take the lead over other branches of civilization. Inventions, exploration, and new knowledge were about to change the course of civilization. Yet this amazing development had its roots in earlier experiments in culture and civilization. These experiments can be traced back 5,500 years to the river valleys of ancient Mesopotamia.

GLOSSARY

Some words have many meanings. This list gives only the meanings of the words as they are used in this book. To find other meanings of these words, look them up in a dictionary.

Abu Bekr: follower of Muhammad; the first caliph.

Age of Faith: another name for the Middle Ages.

alchemy: the science studied by Arab scientists who wanted to turn tin and lead into gold.

algebra: branch of mathematics developed by Arabs.

Allah: the Arabic name for God.

alms: a gift of money, animals, or grain to help the poor.

Arab: a person who speaks Arabic as his native language. Most, but not all, Arabs are Muslims.

Arabic: the language of the Arabs.

armor: iron suits worn by knights and their horses for protection.

astronomy: the science that deals with the sun, moon, stars, and planets.

banking system: method of lending and borrowing capital and establishing credit.

barbarians: people who live on the edges of civilization and want to share in the good things of civilized living.

battering rams: siege weapons; large, thick wooden poles used to break through gates to an enemy city.

bazaar: the Arab marketplace.

Bedouin: Arab nomads.

Berbers: nomadic Muslims from North Africa who destroyed Ghana.

booty: goods taken from the defeated enemy in war.

buttress: a strong stone support used especially to prop up walls of Gothic cathedrals.

Byzantine Empire: the Roman Empire in the East, which lasted until 1453.

caliphs: rulers of Islam; Muhammad's successors.

capital: money or goods that can be invested to make more money.

caravan: a group of people traveling together, using camels to carry them and their goods.

catapults: large siege weapons used to hurl rocks at walls.

Charlemagne: (A.D. 742–814) creator of the Holy Roman Empire.

chivalry: the way of life of medieval knights. Chivalry was the beginning of our ideas of good manners.

Christendom: the area from Constantinople to the Atlantic Ocean, in which Christianity was practiced; Europe in the Middle Ages.

city-state: a city plus the land around it that is under the same political control.

civilization: a condition of life in which a people have a surplus of goods, a division of labor, and cities.

classical civilization: the period c. 500 B.C. to A.D. 500, when Greek and Roman cultures were very important.

clergy: officers of the church.

coat-of-arms: the design on a knight's shield that identified him.

controlling ideas: ideas that control or direct the way a person acts.

convent: home of nuns.

Crusades: eight holy wars fought by Western Europeans against the Muslims between 1096 and 1274. "Crusade" means "War for the Cross."

culture: the traditions and customs of a people; their way of life.

Dark Ages: the early part of the Middle Ages, c. A.D. 500–1000.

Day of Judgment: in Jewish, Christian, and Muslim tradition the end of the world when good men will be rewarded and bad men punished.

desert: an area in which there is not much rainfall and in which few, if any, plants can survive.

division of labor: a separation of workers into different jobs so that more and better goods can be produced.

export tax: fee paid on goods sent out of a country.

fasting: going without food or drink. During Ramadan, from sunrise to sunset, Muslims eat, drink, and smoke nothing. Christians and Jews also observe periods of fasting.

feudal system: Social, political, and economic system of Western Europe in the Middle Ages. It was based on the ownership of land. In return for land, knights paid military service to their lords.

fief: under the feudal system, a piece of land granted by a lord to a knight.

firearm: a weapon from which an object is fired by gunpowder.

fortified: defended against attack.

friars: Christian monks who worked and taught among the people.

generation: all the people born at about the same time. Generations are about 25–30 years apart.

Genghis Khan: the Mongol leader who united the Mongol tribes and conquered more territory than any other man in history.

Gobi Desert: large desert in central Asia that covers one-third of Mongolia.

Gothic architecture: a medieval style of building that "reached toward heaven." Main features were buttresses and pointed arches.

Great Wall: 1,500-mile-long barrier built by the Chinese to keep the barbarians out of China.

Greco-Roman: a term used to identify ideas and customs in Western culture that come from ancient Greece and Rome.

Hegira: the secret journey of Muhammad and Abu Bekr from Mecca to Medina.

heritage: ideas, practices and beliefs handed down from one's ancestors.

historical period: a part of history. We divide history into parts to make it easier to classify and study events.

holy war: war of Muhammad against the enemies of Allah.

import tax: fee paid on goods brought into a country.

irrigation: method of supplying the land with water by artificial means, such as ditches, channels, canals.

Islam: a great monotheistic religion. "Islam" means "surrender" in Arabic. Islam was founded by Muhammad about A.D. 610.

Islamic Empire: the empire in the Middle East built by the Arabs after the death of Muhammad in A.D. 632. It began to decline in the eleventh century.

Jerusalem: city in Palestine that the Crusaders set out to recapture from the Muslims in 1096.

Jews: people who practice Judaism.

Judeo-Christian: a term used to identify ideas and customs in Western culture that come from Jews and Christians.

Kaaba: cube-shaped building in Mecca that contains the holy Black Stone of the Muslims.

knight: a medieval, heavily armored soldier trained to fight on horseback.

Koran: the holy book of Islam. It contains Muhammad's teachings (Allah's messages to him).

Kublai Khan: the last great Mongol khan, who completed the Mongolian conquest of China and established his capital at Peking. He was a grandson of Genghis Khan and ruled from 1260 to 1294.

lance: a long, heavy spear used by medieval knights.

latitude: distance in degrees north and south of the equator.

longitude: distance in degrees east and west of the prime meridian.

lord: powerful landowner in the feudal system.

Magna Carta: a charter of the rights of Englishmen signed by King John in 1215. "Magna Carta" means "Great Charter."

manor: the land controlled by one knight or squire and farmed by the peasants of one village.

Mecca: the holy city of the Muslims. All Muslim men are supposed to make at least one pilgrimage to Mecca. Muhammad was born in Mecca.

medieval: of the Middle Ages. The time when Judeo-Christian ideas were most important to Western men. The Middle Ages, or the Age of Faith, includes the period of European history c. A.D. 500 to 1500.

Medina: city where Muhammad taught about Islam.

medium of exchange: money, which may be things other than coins or notes.

Mesopotamia: land between the Tigris and Euphrates Rivers; now part of Iraq.

Middle Ages: the medieval period; the period of European history from c. A.D. 500 to 1500.

Middle East: region of the world that joins the two landmasses of Africa and Eurasia; often called the "crossroads" of the world.

middleman: trader who makes a profit by buying goods from one man and reselling them to another.

mission: one's purpose in life.

moldboard: the part of a plow attached to the plowshare that turns the soil to the side of the furrows.

monarchy: a form of government in which one person rules, for example, a king or queen.

monastery: home of monks.

money-and-market economy: an economic system with capital, investment, division of labor, wages, and profits; prices and products depend on demand and supply in the market.

Mongols: nomadic barbarians of east central Asia who built the largest land empire in the history of the world, in the thirteenth century. It was also one of the shortest-lived empires.

monk: man who belongs to a religious order.

monotheism: belief in one God.

mosque: Muslim place of worship.

Muhammad: the founder of Islam. He was born about A.D. 570 in Mecca and died in 632.

Muslims: the followers of Muhammad; people who practice the religion of Islam. Muslim (sometimes spelled Moslem) means "one who surrenders" his life and thoughts to the will of God.

nobles: members of the ruling class in Latin Christendom; lords and ladies.

nomads: people who move from place to place and do not settle down.

nun: woman who belongs to a religious order.

oasis: a fertile spot in a desert.

Ogdai Khan: son and successor of Genghis Khan who began the second wave of Mongol conquests.

paradise: heaven.

parallel: things or events that are alike in most ways, but develop or happen independently.

parliament: in Western Europe, a council of representatives of the noblemen, clergy, knights, and townsmen.

patriotic: showing love or devotion to one's country.

patriotism: love of, or devotion to, one's country.

peasants: farmers in the Middle Ages who were protected by knights. They worked for the knights and supplied them with food.

Peking: Chinese city chosen by Kublai Khan as his capital.

peninsula: a portion of land surrounded by water on three sides.

pilgrimage: a trip to a religious shrine or holy place.

plowshare: part of a moldboard plow that cuts a furrow.

pope: highest officer of the Roman Catholic Church.

profit: money over and above the amount spent on or invested in a project.

prophet: a religious leader inspired by a divine power; one who foretells or predicts the future.

Ramadan: the Muslim month of fasting.

religious order: a society or group of monks or nuns.

Renaissance: the time of the "rebirth" of interest in the traditions, learning, and culture of the Greeks and Romans.

representative government: government in which people can make their wishes known to their rulers.

savanna: treeless plain.

sequential: events that follow other events, and may be caused by them.

siege warfare: a military tactic in which an army surrounds an enemy city, cutting the city off from food supplies and forcing it to surrender.

sifr: the Arabic word for cipher, or zero.

silent barter: the way gold was traded in medieval African kingdoms; done in a way so that neither side ever talked to the other.

sin: breaking God's laws.

sisters of mercy: nuns who worked and taught among the people.

stained glass: colored glass used in the windows of Gothic cathedrals. Most stained glass windows pictured scenes from the Bible.

steppes: grassy plains; prairie.

stirrup: attachment to a saddle; the stirrup holds a rider's feet and helps him to stay on his horse.

stone-gods: gods worshipped by Arabs before the founding of Islam.

subsist: stay alive.

subsistence agriculture: agriculture that does not produce a food surplus.

subsistence economy: a condition of life in which people produce just enough goods and services to stay alive. They produce no surplus.

Sudan: wide belt of grassland south of the Sahara.

Sumer: the land between the Tigris and Euphrates Rivers where scholars believe civilization began.

surplus: a quantity or amount over and above what the producers need for themselves.

tension: a state of unrest.

tournament: contest between two groups of medieval knights.

trend: general direction or development.

tribute: taxes paid to a foreign government.

vassal: one under the protection of someone else.

wadis: dry river beds in Arabia used as roads by camel caravans.

INDEX